"Peace by Piece is so beautifully transparent. It inspires a new-found love for the Father and how He is so powerfully able and willing to give us beauty for ashes. Nicole is down to earth and relatable, it's almost as if you are walking through each experience right there with her. I highly recommend this to believers and non-believers alike. What a wonderful read!"

–**Natasha Grantz**, author of "A Changed Heart"

"This is a book from the heart! Nicole has a way of bringing you into her life's struggles, tragic moments, and day to day difficulties only to come away with greater understanding and freedom found in Christ. Peace by Piece is a testimony of God's healing, faithfulness and love to be found by each of us who travel through the ups and downs of life. She found the answer to every need in Jesus and her assurance of His powerful healing presence is woven through the words of her book. This is an honest and compelling story of Nicole's journey to finding peace, and it is a story of hope and healing for everyone who reads it."

–**Brenda Newport**, Former Executive Director,
Women's Care Center of Erie County

"As Nicole gathers the pieces of her life from that broken road, she faces off with some common fears and the nagging feeling of loss to live a life totally sold out to God. The reader can learn the friendship of Jesus and gain hope for what God has for each of us along the way."

–**Janelle Keith**, speaker and author of "Grace for Your Waist"

Nicole Drayer

SURRENDERING ALL THAT IS
BEAUTIFULLY BROKEN

NICOLE DRAYER

Nicole Drayer

Woven Books
YOUR STORY. HIS GLORY.

Peace by Piece: *Surrendering All that is Beautifully Broken*
Published by Woven Books | www.wovenbooks.com
Cover and Interior Design by Dawn Estela

With Gratitude

This book is dedicated to my loving husband, Greg, to my three beautiful children, and to my ever-supportive parents.

Greg, you are my ultimate blessing. God gave you to me in college and showed me what it was like to be truly respected and properly courted in a Godly dating relationship. You have always loved me with a Christ-like love, putting my needs above your own. You are my best friend and biggest fan. You have always encouraged, prayed for, helped, and believed in me ... even when I did not believe in myself. I can never thank you enough for holding down the fort and praying for me while I took time away to obey God's call to write this book. I love you more.

Caleb, Eden, and Eli, you are my greatest and most special gifts of all. God blessed me with three amazing children! You are all smart, kind, respectful, and each gifted with special talents. My prayer has always been that God would protect you physically, emotionally, and spiritually. Also, that you would know Jesus and be known by Him. As you move forward on your life's journey, I pray that you grow ever closer to Him, be obedient to the call on each of your lives, and that you, too, would let the peace of Christ rule in your hearts. I love you all so much!

Mom and Dad, you have shown me an unconditional love that I never understood until I had children of my own. I want to thank you always for your support and prayers. Being a family in ministry, you've always been there—more than willing to help—if we had a need. Thank you for being my role models and for your love. I can only hope to be the kind of loyal and caring parents to my own children as you have been to me. I love you both very much.

I would like to especially thank the Lord for blessing me with an absolutely amazing publishing team at Woven Books. These three beautiful Godly women were brought into my life at exactly the right time in my writing journey—when I wasn't sure what was next. God hand-picked Lori, Janelle, and Dawn and planted them in my life as an answer to prayer. These wise and talented women have prayed for, supported, and encouraged me every step of the way, and I am truly grateful. They have been a true inspiration and blessing. Thank you, my dear sweet sisters in Christ!

I cannot imagine completing this book without giving ALL of the glory to my Father God! You are my Rock, Redeemer, Savior, Friend, Constant, Shield, Joy, and Peace. You are Life and Truth. You are Love and Grace. I would not be who I am, and this book would not have been accomplished if it were not for You. I praise you for not giving up on me and for nudging and guiding me through this entire arduous process. I praise YOU for who You are and for what You want to say through my story. May many be encouraged by the saving hope of Jesus Christ. Thank you, beautiful Prince of Peace, Amen!

Foreword

After meditating on my Bible study notes over a span of six months, God gave me the message for this book. As I searched through my ink-filled journals, there was a common thread throughout my time of study, thankfulness, and prayer. It was a theme 15 years in the making as I received my call to write: God the Father and Jesus were *my Peace*.

The first time I became a mother was the initial moment I submitted to the Lord's prompting. Our firstborn son, Caleb, was our promise—our call confirmed to raise up a heritage of believers. I can remember that night like it was yesterday. I was a young first-time mom, rocking my beautiful baby boy back to sleep in the middle of the night. We were the only two awake. As I held Caleb and prayed for him, I had such a peace. I wanted that moment to last forever and etched it in my mind and on my heart. Then, the Lord revealed something to me. So, after I laid Caleb down for the remainder of the night, I grabbed a pen and wrote these words ...

> As I sit in my newborn son's room at 4:00 am and reflect on my life, God is revealing to me what a beautiful creation of His I truly am and what a strong, courageous, and bold woman He has made me. Through each phase of my life, God has deeply touched me and strengthened my faith. He has taught me to give up self, give up control, give up the pieces of my life—my pain, my fears—and let Him heal me, set me free, and be Lord of my life. He has helped me allow

Him into the deep places of my soul and heart to cleanse me, change me, strengthen me, and grow me. Through all of this, I am finally learning to accept and embrace one of the most beautiful gifts God offers His children–inner peace.

Since then, our family and responsibilities have grown. And life has a way of always being busy and chaotic. But Jesus is always my Peace. Even though I once lived as a slave to anxiety and stress, Jesus was my Peace. Throughout both good and bad adventures, Jesus was, and still is, my Peace.

The more we surrender and give up the pieces of our lives that we hold so tightly to, the more peace we feel. The more we become like Jesus and the person He created us to be, the clearer our call becomes. The more we understand the Lord's work, the more our earthly passions dissipate. And His ways, His plans, His purposes, and His desires become our new passion and reason for being.

How can this be? How does this occur? I don't know about you, but I don't always act like the Christian woman I am called to be—in total and complete surrender to Christ—or have a calm spirit all the time. I just know that *He was, still is, and will always be my Peace. No matter what!*

The chapters that follow are a compilation of stories from my life's journey thus far and the many lessons our Mighty God has taught me along the way. My prayer is that you, too, will live *Peace by Piece.*

Living Peace by Piece is:

Forgiveness   A Heart Issue

DISCIPLESHIP   FOCUS   SERVING   SACRIFICE

HARD WORK   Freedom   TO BE CHRIST-LIKE

Loving Others   Courage   HEALING   Faith

VICTORY   Jesus First   Commitment   WISDOM

Constant Surrender   Sanctification

OBEDIENCE   LETTING GO   SELF DENIAL

Fruit Bearing   Being led by the Holy Spirit   Suffering

SATISFYING TO THE SOUL

Prayer   Disciple-Making   TRUTH

Awareness

A Journey   A Process

SALVATION

Repentance

JOY

Chapter 1
The Pieces of My Past

I was 19 years old. Sitting alone in my room, I was at the lowest point in my life. There I sat, depressed, empty, my soul brimming with despair and grief. You see, my parents had picked me up from college after receiving a terrifying phone call from my roommates, telling them I had attempted to end my life.

I had nobody to turn to. Nobody could possibly understand the pain I felt. But there I was—sitting on my bed, holding a small Gideon Bible in my hands. I don't even remember where it came from. Until this point, I did not even know Jesus. I believed in Him and knew about him, but didn't have a living, breathing relationship with Him. I was terrified of God because I was immersed in a sinful lifestyle and only learned about His wrath. I never really heard about His mighty love and endless grace.

I had been making one poor decision after another since the time I entered high school, which in turn caused me to spiral downward to the bottom of this deep, dark pit. I knew I was going to hell and didn't think there was hope for me, which paralyzed me with agonizing fear. I hated myself and who I had become. It was then that the Lord began to pursue me. Or had He been pursuing me all along?

The Pieces of
Childhood Memories and Fears

In order to better understand what drove me to this point in life, we need to dig a little deeper into my childhood.

I was born the youngest of four children. A shy and quiet child with long curly brown hair, I was often referred to as "the baby." It's a title that carries with me to this day. Yes, even as a grown woman, I am still my parent's baby. I must admit that I secretly like being the youngest. However, according to child psychology and birth order research, I was sort of the "youngest-only child." My brother and two sisters are much older than me, so I exhibit characteristics of an only child as well. At times, I like to refer to myself as the "oops" baby! I may not have been planned, but I always knew that I was very much loved. As a result of my birth order, I naturally felt a distance between my siblings and me during my younger years.

I grew up in a small steel mill town along the Allegheny River in a suburb of Pittsburgh, Pennsylvania. So, for almost a decade, I resided with my mom and dad, two sisters, one brother, my pap, and great uncle. We lived in an old red brick duplex together, the home where my mother grew up, and life was good! For a while.

My dad, the encourager and peacemaker, worked most of the time to provide for his family. My mom, the nurturer and homemaker, stayed at home to take care of us while we were little, but eventually went back to work. My brother, two sisters, and I had a stable family life growing up. I have fond memories of family vacations, birthday parties, large holiday celebrations, and summer picnics.

During this time, I was closest to my oldest sister, who was like a second mother to me. My brother looked out for me as much as he could, and my other sister, well we didn't get along too well. But now she is one of my dearest friends. Honestly, if I can be devoted to and care for my family the way in which my parents unconditionally adored my siblings and me, then I'll know half of my job is complete.

We were a strong Catholic family with a Polish, Italian, and Slovak heritage. We hardly ever missed one Sunday Mass, one Catechism class, one confession, or the making of any sacraments. So, I grew up with a belief in God. I believed that

God and Jesus were real and that they loved me. However, there was a disconnect for me. I didn't comprehend who God truly was and who I was in His eyes; my heart was so very empty. My young life continued to flood with trepidations and misunderstandings, and I began to fill the void with temporary things that did not satisfy. I struggled to stay afloat and make it through the rough waters ahead.

What I didn't know then (but is evident now), was that I was a child full of many insecurities and fears. Had counseling been as common then as it is now, I'm pretty sure I would have seen a therapist as a little girl. I was afraid of death and darkness. You may think that's standard for most kids.

My concerns, however, were extreme for such a young heart. Lying awake at night, I'd fixate on death and become flooded with anxiety and emotion. Panic-stricken, my heart would beat rapidly, and I would begin to sweat. I dwelled on death so much that I wondered if death led to ... NOTHING ... only darkness with no memory of anything at all. As I held my thoughts captive on that horrid feeling of nothingness ... I was paralyzed with terror.

Nightmares became the norm, and I grew to loathe bedtime. I despised sleeping in my own room. I shared an area with my older brother due to the size of our modest home. My half was cute and girly. His half looked much like an older brother of eight years should have ... complete with Ozzy Osborne albums and Pink Floyd posters. However, it's also why I spent most nights nestled on my parent's floor—until I was almost 12!

I missed out on many slumber parties until the age of 13 or 14 because I was nervous to sleep over at any friends' homes. My rationale was that something awful would happen to my parents when I was away, and I might never see them again. The longing and emptiness were real.

As I grew up, I was often referred to as my mother's "shadow." I was so attached to my mom, that wherever she went, you can sure bet I followed. If she went down to the basement to do laundry, so did I. If she went upstairs to put clothes away, so did I. If she went outside ... well, you know the rest! I had a strong need and desire to be with her  all the time. Most of my summer days were spent either playing alone or with a neighborhood friend or two, sitting by my mom's side, or with my pap. I loved my pap so very much. I developed a strong relationship with my grandfather because he cared for me while my parents worked and my siblings were occupied with their lives full of part-time jobs and school activities.

My days with pap were the best! We cooked, watched "The Young and the Restless" *(his favorite soap opera)*, and either sat on the front porch counting loud dusty mill trucks or swayed on the glider in the back yard watching boats on the glistening Allegheny River. My favorite activity of all was when we would take a leisurely drive to the country for a mushroom picking adventure.

Sadly, our days were cut short; my pap died when I was only 12 years old. Oh, how I missed him. I was so deeply saddened when he passed; it took me quite some time to get over the loss.

When Kindergarten began, excitement to start school soon turned to devastation for me. I'll never forget the moment it was time for my mom to exit the classroom. She had to pull away from our warm embrace, turn around, and LEAVE! I cried and cried. Weeping and grieving this loss of home—*and all that I ever knew*—did not end until sometime after Christmas that year.

Although I made new friends and settled down some, new uncertainties developed. I was now intimidated by the school principal and the scary dungeon-like bathrooms. As a result of avoiding the frightening restrooms at any cost, I wet my pants in front of all my classmates. What a memory! Fresh fears and insecurities surfaced daily.

The Pieces of Adolescent Insecurities:
Always the Alternate

It was a long, hot summer before my 5th grade year, and I worked so very hard yet again. I practiced skills and techniques over and over with a more experienced teenage family friend. After I gave it my absolute all, the results were in. *Alternate.* Dreadful words to my ears. I made the position of alternate cheerleader for our Little League squad. *Again.*

My heart sunk as I had to wear the ridiculously ugly green and white sweater, complete with hideous shorts. I stood out like a sore thumb while the other more talented and pretty girls donned beautiful matching yellow and green sweaters and cute little skirts. It was an outfit I longed to own and wear.

You see, the *alternate* cheerleader was expected to attend every single practice and learn each routine with the hope ... *oops, did I say hope?* With the *chance* that one cheerleader just might be ill enough to miss a game. Then I could get out of the bleachers and have a golden moment on the field as a real cheerleader! *Alternate.* Oh, the humiliation of a young girl's heart. Have you ever felt like an alternate? Second best? A replacement? Not good enough? I sure have.

As many of us experience, the transition to junior high was extremely difficult. My group of best childhood friends was altered. My cute porcelain skin, big brown eyes, and bouncy little girl curls morphed into an awkward haircut, metal braces, very large glasses, and a ruddy complexion. I struggled with my unpleasant exterior and finding my place.

7

With low self-esteem, I had this deep desire to please my friends much more than my parents or God, leading to many self-destructive behaviors. Those years were full of loneliness, as I felt ugly and unimportant. *An alternate.* The rejection I experienced had a greater impact on me throughout life than I ever could have imagined. Adolescent inadequacies coupled with my childhood fears equaled hopelessness and desperation for me. I was determined to fit back in with my popular group of friends, the ones I once enjoyed life with throughout my elementary years. No matter what.

As I matured into high school, things became different as my physical appearance transformed again. This time my image changed to what the world would see as more pleasing. My hair grew in, and I modeled a short curly bob. It was time for contact lenses, and my braces finally came off. The most exciting thing to me? At the beginning of the school year, my mom let me choose a whole new wardrobe ... *by myself!* I always admired my big sister who was in college, and I wanted to wear cool clothes like her and her stylish friends.

From their example, I became curious about new trends and enjoyed tasteful fashion. In addition, my many hours of hard work and practice paid off, and I made the junior varsity cheerleading squad. Guess what? People began to notice me again; my social status began to change, but so did my behaviors. Although my looks became more pleasing, my actions were not very becoming at all.

I had a deep need to not only fit in, but to also have a boyfriend and feel attractive. Somehow in my teenage brain, I thought true love and acceptance meant having a significant other. That it would make me important, confident, and high up on the status quo. Throughout this phase in my life, I believed I was *"in love"* at least once, had a few crushes, and my heart-strings were pulled in many different directions because of unwise decisions. The only relationships I experienced in high school—*and even throughout college*—were sinful, unhealthy, and codependent.

Wanting so desperately to be loved and noticed, I chased after guys who were prideful and manipulative. For me, there was some thrill in the chase and found satisfaction in the catch; however, the end result was even more emptiness. These relationships were not real love. They were selfish and sick. I was abused emotionally, neglected, and was always left alone with a broken heart. All of these associations were based on underage drinking and sex. From the time I entered high school, I lived a double life. My family saw me as one way and my friends saw me another. God, however, saw every step.

The Pieces of College Catastrophes

The car was jam-packed and ready to be unloaded at the busy and chaotic dorm—my new home for the next four years. As my parents were ready to leave me at Edinboro University, where I would study elementary and special education, my childhood fears of separation anxiety surfaced once again. I was full of deep sorrow to grow-up and begin a new life. My heart ached as I said good-bye to my loving family. It should have been an exciting time, full of adventure and growth, but

9

not for me. I was depressed because I had to find my place and try to fit in all over again.

I went home many weekends during my sad and lonely college days. I only wanted to be home, safe and sound. No pressure to be someone I was not. No struggles to fit in to a place that I did not like one bit. No temptations to fight against daily. However, being the *"follower"* that I was, I quickly got sucked into the partying lifestyle during the days I remained on campus. This was where the real trouble began.

One evening, my friends and I received a visit from one of my high-school friends who went to a nearby college. He was smart, funny, and the life of the party. Everyone was drawn to him. He partied with us, and before I knew it, I was dating him. Might I add that he was best friends with a boy who I *thought* was my first love in middle school—a boy who never treated me with dignity or respect. A boy I still had feelings for. And now I allowed myself to enter yet another unhealthy and sinful relationship—dating the best friend of my old boyfriend! Not a very good foundation at all. Without an understanding of what real love was, it quickly became a relationship full of lust, jealousy, codependency, and obsession.

The Pieces of My Brokenness and Shame

It was an August evening when we drove to a nearby restaurant. He sat in the car, and I went inside and timidly snuck into the bathroom. I took care of what I had to, and returned to his car. We both trembled with fear as I pulled out the pregnancy test. As we gazed at the two red lines, I crumbled. It was positive. I knew for the past several weeks; it was a feeling in my gut—literally—as I felt nauseous and moody. I tried to deny it. But here, truth stared us right in the face. We both sobbed and sobbed. I felt so afraid, helpless, and full of utter despair.

In just a few weeks, I was returning to college. I was going to school to become a teacher—something I had always dreamed of. This ugly side of my life was hidden from my parents. What would they think? How would they respond? As a people-pleaser, it grieved me to know that I was about to disappoint and hurt my parents in such a profound way. They were the only two people that supported and loved me most. What was I going to do? I came from a good family who was paying for my college education. I was raised in a church ... *so what was happening? What did I do? What do I do now?* Such utter confusion, chaos, and turmoil flooded my life in the form of those two straight red lines.

I kept this secret buried as I went back to college. I tried to mask the confusion and despair that consumed me. You see, I love children. I always have. Since I was a little girl, I wanted a family of my own. I had my dreams all planned out, complete with a good husband, four or five children (maybe one adopted), a house with a white picket fence, a dog, and me working as an elementary school teacher. Now everything was ruined. Everything was out of order. Now the dream was destroyed. Because I loved and valued life, I loved this baby growing inside of me. I was so sad yet desperately tried to protect that which was in me. I talked and cried to my precious child, and simply did not know what to do.

By *not* making a decision, in reality I was making a decision as the life within me grew over time. I was carrying the heaviest burden ever. I knew that abortion was ending a life and not pleasing to God. However, I was too afraid to face my parents, family, and society with the news: *I was an utter failure.* I was living a nightmare and wanted so badly to wake up. I wished that I could turn back time and do things differently. But I couldn't.

After many agonizing hours of contemplation, weeping, and dread, the baby's father and I decided to abort. We were not 100 percent certain it was the right decision as we wrestled through options, but it was made in complete desperation. So young and naïve. This day was my absolute lowest. A day that I despise, even today, as I write these words. A day that remains hauntingly vivid.

Throughout the entire abortion process I wanted to yell *STOP!* But I didn't. I cried out to God for mercy and left the clinic empty and numb.

Chapter 2
The Pieces of My Heart

I don't know if I would have gone through with suicide or if it was a simple cry for help. I had to do something. I felt like I was standing in the middle of a room, screaming at the top of my lungs, for someone to rescue me. But nobody saw or heard. The thought of ending my life was on the forefront of my mind because I could not take the heaviness or pain anymore. The guilt, the shame, the secret I had to live with. I felt as if I were wearing a scarlet letter. If anyone mentioned babies or abortion, I felt like every person in the room was pointing fingers at me. It was a burden I had to bare.

I crept into the bathroom of our campus apartment and stared straight at myself in the mirror. I trembled, cried, then picked up a razor and fell to the floor. I gripped the blade, pressed it against my wrist, and tried to scrape the skin where my vein was. I thought for sure I locked the door. But at that very moment, one of my roommates entered the bathroom. I remember her forcefully yelling for me to stop and calling out to our other friends. Before I knew it, my family was contacted and immediately rushed two hours to get to the school. My parents, not knowing what to do or what was going on, brought me home. And I had no desire to return.

〜〜〜

"The Lord Jesus pierced the darkness in my soul and life and pulled me out of the slimy pit of despair."

This brings us back to my bedroom. Me, alone, with the tiny green Gideon Bible. I was in the comfort of my own home, surrounded by those who loved me. Yet, as I sat on my bed, I felt the darkness of depression weigh heavily on my heart; I despised myself and my life. I knew that I was going to hell and wanted to die, to the point of almost ending my life. The abortion triggered Post Traumatic Stress Disorder, and so much anger and self-hatred filled every inch of my being. I dismissed any desire to live and be happy.

Despite all these horrifying memories swirling around in my brain ... *in one critical moment* I opened the little green Bible and saw a short prayer written inside of it. A prayer of salvation.

After reading it a few times, I felt the hopelessness melting off of my heart, and I knew I had to immediately kneel down and cry out to God. I didn't say it just once, but many times. It was an intimate time of true confession with a promise of forgiveness. I prayed that prayer of surrender with a deep sincerity and desperation like never before. I then wrote my name in the Bible and dated it. From that moment on, my new journey began. My eyes were opened, and I could now see! *Truly see!* It was as if I had lived with blinders on until this life-changing point.

Hope in the Brokenness

After giving my life to Christ, I felt so relieved, forgiven, and set free—something I never experienced before. My mighty God saved me! I didn't understand how He could forgive and forget my wrongdoings. What kind of amazing love was this? I simply did not understand, but was so full of awe and gratitude. Just as it is written in Psalm 40:2,

> *"He lifted me out of the slimy pit, out of the*
> *mud and mire; He set my feet on a rock and*
> *gave me a firm place to stand."*

This was the first step of my journey—*when I met my Jesus!* I gave Him my heart, and I was born again. The Lord Jesus pierced the darkness in my soul and life and pulled me out of the slimy pit of despair. He put my feet on solid ground. He rescued me from myself. He forgave me, transformed me, and healed this broken heart. He made me whole and new and gave me hope.

In the days that followed, I read many different scriptures that I could not fully understand or comprehend. However, certain words were so timely; they blew my mind because I was never exposed to them before. Because of the depths of my dark and sinful lifestyle that filled me with guilt and shame, these words were a source of both comfort and healing. They were truth and life— *words that set me free.* Let them soothe your soul right now:

"For as the heavens are high above the earth,
so great is His mercy toward those who fear
Him; As far as the east is from the west, so far
has He removed our transgressions from us."
(Psalm 103:11-12)

"I, even I, am He who blots out your
transgressions for My own sake; And I will not
remember your sins." (Isaiah 43:25)

I write all of this to tell you there is *always* hope. There *IS* light at the end of the dark tunnel. Whether you are going through trials brought on by your own human sin and pride or if they are brought through other circumstances, God *IS* with *YOU!* There is no sin that He cannot forgive. None. He died for all! His blood IS enough. He suffered for our sake. There is a way to live in peace and forgiveness with the Father.

Dear friend, never give up searching desperately for Him. He is there patiently waiting for you to love, comfort, heal, and forgive you.

In John 8:12, Jesus says,

"I am the light of the world.
Whoever follows me will not walk in darkness
but will have the light of life."

And Isaiah 40:31 proclaims,

"...but those who hope in the Lord shall renew
their strength. They shall mount up on wings
like eagles; they shall run and not be weary,
they will walk and not faint."

There is a song by worship artist Kari Jobe called *The Garden*, and it is a song of hope. The lyrics go like this:

"I can see the ivy growing through the wall, 'cause you will stop at nothing to heal my broken soul. Faith is rising up like ivy, reaching for the light. Hope is stirring deep inside me, making all things right. Love is lifting me from sorrow catching every tear, dispelling every lie and torment crushing all my fears."

Thank you, Jesus, for catching every tear because of your great and mighty love and care for us.

The moment I gave my life to the Lord, it became a joyous occasion. I felt new and different and had a desire to live life again. I was on fire for God and learned and grew in so many ways. Things I never knew or understood now made sense. I believe this can happen for you, too. The Holy Spirit comes into your life and begins to help, guide, and steer you towards the Father. John 14:26 says,

> *"But the Helper, the Holy Spirit, whom the*
> *Father will send in My name, He will teach*
> *you all things, and bring to your*
> *remembrance all things that I said to you."*

Misplaced Pieces

My friend, the moment you surrender to Christ and first realize the need for a Savior, He takes over. Your new journey begins as the Holy Spirit then takes residency in your heart. Sanctification *(the act of cleansing to make Holy)* begins, and the Lord changes you from the inside out.

But, let's be honest with each other—*life is messy*, and there are some pieces of life that are so hard to let go of. After asking God to take over, we subtly take pieces back over time and hold onto them very tightly. We think we can give God a little bit and keep the rest for ourselves. Discontentment sets in. Happiness fades. We feel far from God.

A verse I meditated on while writing this book was Colossians 3:15:

> *"And let the peace of God rule in your hearts,*
> *to which also you were called in one body; and*
> *be thankful."*

Notice the verse says, *"Let the peace of God rule in your hearts."* You must *let* it. *"It"* being the peace of Christ—*not let the "piece of you"*—rule in your heart. This means that Jesus is in control of your heart when you are in close relationship with Him. Jesus rules ... every single piece. But because of our sinful and selfish natures, we take pieces back and hold onto them. We think we can handle them and do a better job than God. Like a little child who won't share a toy, we defiantly shout *"It's mine!"* When this happens, *we* try to rule parts of our hearts and not let Christ be the true Lord of our lives. This causes frustration, confusion, and lack of peace.

What pieces of your heart have you taken back from God? What is causing division between you and your Savior? Those things become idols because you count them as more important than God. I know I struggle with this very issue in my own life over and over.

Somehow, through our Christian walk, we tend to let other passions slip in and replace God as our focus. If we are not alert, on guard, and living an active faith, we end up serving *"self"* instead of Jesus. We do not give Him everything and instead build up idols of our own selfish desires, agendas, decisions, control, time, personal problems, devices, and reputation. We are commanded to:

> *"'Love the LORD your God with all your heart,*
> *with all your soul, with all your strength, and*
> *with all your mind,' and 'your neighbor as*
> *yourself.'"* (Luke 10:27)

How can you love God with all of your heart when you hold tightly to so many of the pieces of your heart and don't completely trust Him to rule your heart?

Get Right with God: Surrender It All!

Has your life been too much about you? Perhaps your past? Your brokenness and shame? Control? Perfectionism? Materialism? Family? Your schedule? Eating habits? Your phone? Social media? Your language? Your attitude? Your marriage? Your thoughts? Your addictions?

The only way to loosen your tight, white-knuckled grip on the pieces of your heart is to do what I did that day in my bedroom. *Surrender.* Ask the Lord to forgive your disobedience. If you've never yielded your life at all to the Lord, or if you feel God stirring your heart to return to faith ... now is your time. Ask for forgiveness, and tell Jesus how lost you've been without Him. Give Him your life, your past, your heart, your all. Jesus is calling you ... *won't you answer?* Just like that simple prayer in my little green Gideon Bible, won't you please search from deep within and pray this prayer with me?

> Lord Jesus, I come to you as I am. I am a broken mess. I realize that I can no longer do life on my own. I am in desperate need of you. Please forgive me for all of the sin in my life. Forgive everything I have done to hurt you, others, or myself. I want to change and be made new. Thank you for dying on

the cross to take away my sin. Thank you for making a way that I can be restored to Father God. Thank you for suffering for me. I accept you as my Lord and Savior. Please send your Holy Spirit into my life to teach and guide me. Help me to be the person you called me to be. Help me to heal from my past and to live for you. I want to serve you and help others. I excitedly look to the future with hope, knowing that you are always with me and will carry me through both good days and bad. I surrender all of my life and my heart to you. Please restore that which is broken and make me whole. Use me for your glory, I pray. I love you. In Jesus' Name, Amen!

Today's Date:

_____

Now you can return to this prayer and remember what the Lord has done. You can remember when you took a step closer to the Lord, and He continued to sanctify you and draw you near.

"I am the way and the truth and the life. No one comes to the Father except through me."
(John 14:6)

Nicole Drayer

Chapter 3
The Pieces of My Desires

I mustered what little nerve I had that morning and called my college advisor and favorite professor, Dr. Ruth Nash-Thompson, to tell her I wasn't returning for the next semester. How could I, after what happened?

Dr. Thompson was an intelligent, bold, and beautiful woman with a great sense of humor. But during this time in my life, I was fragile, unconfident, scared, and not the least bit assertive. My parents were prepared to move me back home for good.

"My little fluffers," she began. ("Little fluffers" was a pet name she used for some of her students—me included.) *"Yes, you are coming back because I will be here for you. I believe in you."*

Four words. That's all it took to convince me to continue my education. Positive words of encouragement and life from someone I trusted and admired. I praise God for not only saving my lost soul, but also for putting this beautiful woman in my life who believed in me ... *at just the right moment.* And it was the best decision I could've ever made.

Let the Change Begin

So, I settled into school, and was encouraged to find a group of Christians on campus to help me during this time of growth and transition. On Thursday evenings, I attended a worship gathering called University Christian Fellowship (UCF). The very first night I convinced myself to go, I snuck into the back of the room, trying to find a seat by myself. What I saw astonished me! Between 50 and 80 college students gathered to pray, sing songs of worship, perform funny skits, and listen to the word of God. I never heard or sang songs like that before. *Ever!* I sat and cried because every single one of them spoke directly to me. One I clearly remember went like this:

> "As the deer panteth for the water so my soul longeth after thee, you alone are my heart's desire and I long to worship thee. You alone are my strength my shield, to you alone may my spirit yield."

Oh, how I cried as the Lord reached down to touch and comfort me. I was being made new, and it was beautiful. I felt so safe, happy, and inspired at UCF.

However, I had to walk back to my apartment each Thursday after the meeting was done. Don't get me wrong, my roommates had been very good friends to me. God even put one of the girls in the right place at the right time to call my parents after I attempted to take my life. To say I'm forever grateful is an understatement. However, God was changing my heart, and I no longer desired to participate in the things I once lived for. It was like I had my foot in two different worlds. I liked God's world much better.

I felt the pressing need to move out on my own—something I never *ever* would have imagined or done in my own strength. Being the *"baby"* of my family, I admit I was a little spoiled. I was raised in a safe and comforting environment, not to mention I was a *"follower,"* remember? But to live alone? It was a huge step at this point in my young life.

I shared the news with my parents, and although they had not known the root of my despair yet, they sensed my internal struggle between this new and old way of life. They were grateful for the positive changes in me due to this special group of friends from UCF and knew this would be for my benefit. We found a nice private room in a small dorm called Scott Hall. I moved in January, and I can remember the living space as if it were yesterday. It was the last room at the end of the hall of maybe 20 rooms. It was white, small, and very quaint. A simple space, really.

My new living quarters weren't the big difference, though. The music, movies, people, clothes, and everything I once knew were either changed or gone. I didn't watch TV, and I only listened to Christian music. God replaced my old friends with young men and women who were serious about their faith and who could encourage, help, and disciple me.

In God's divine direction, my new dorm room was right next door to a girl from my high school. She gave her life to the Lord as a young girl, but was not active in her faith at the time. While I was learning and growing, she came right alongside me. I found a church near campus where many of my new friends attended. The word of God was taught in a mighty way, and a short time later, I publicly shared my testimony and was baptized.

God drastically changed my desires and wants. I could now stand firm in my faith and not sink. I was joyful. God was transforming me in extreme ways. When I think back, Romans 12:2 comes to mind:

> *"Do not conform to the pattern of this world,*
> *but be transformed by the renewing of your*
> *mind. Then you will be able to test and*
> *approve what God's will is—his good, pleasing*
> *and perfect will."*

Desire for a Significant Other

When I gave my life to Jesus, my last non-Christian dating relationship, with the baby's father, severed for good. It was not a healthy situation for either of us. I was living alone in Scott Hall. My life radically changed, and I felt such an intimacy with the Lord. This was the first time I had ever read the Bible from front cover to back. I didn't completely understand it all, but still took every opportunity to soak up the Word. The Lord also hand-picked and placed older Godly women in my life as mentors to support and encourage me. I never felt judged or scrutinized by them. Only loved and accepted. My desire to have a boyfriend and to be noticed faded. I just wanted Jesus. A friend recommended the book

"*Passion and Purity,*" by Elisabeth Elliot. This book spoke right to me and taught me about real love ... *the way God intended it to be.* If I had love again ... *I wanted to do it right.* I wanted it to be God-honoring. I distinctly remember kneeling down by my bed to pray, saying to the Lord,

> "I give my all to you ... whatever that means. I don't even care if I ever marry. I want to live for only you. If that means being single the rest of my life, then so be it. If you have someone for me, that is great, too. Right now, I want it to be just you and me!"

How did God respond to that prayer of surrender? I began to bump into a guy named Greg at various spots on campus, and he ended up in a few of my small group Bible studies. There was something different about him. You see, Greg knew my past. I revealed to him and a small group of friends how I had been healing from an abortion. They listened and prayed with me. Greg treated me no differently, and I did not understand why. God put a longing in me to get to know this young man. But I was about to graduate in a few days and move back home. Why in the world would God want us to start a relationship when I was moving hours away?

The last night of the semester is quite memorable to me. My friends and I attended a Friday night Bible study at a home near our campus. The house was jammed packed with young adults longing to learn about Jesus.

I wasn't very assertive at all during this time, but I knew in my gut that I *had* to talk to Greg and give him my number. This was absurd to me! I never did anything like this before in my life *(unless I was intoxicated)*. Give a boy my phone number? But I knew I had to, so I did!

He was a drummer in a local Christian band. So, I gave him a little piece of paper with my number and told him to give me a call and let me know how his band was doing. *(I needed some reason to do this crazy gesture!)*

Well, due to my obedience to the Lord, Greg and I have been blessed with 18 years of marriage, have three beautiful children, and live a life of ministry together as he pastors Rolling Hills Church. And, might I add, he still has the little piece of paper with my number on it. Can we all say *"Awwww?"*

Desire to Be Accepted and People Please

I've been a *"follower"* most of my life. Over the past two decades, God has been drastically altering that part of me. Ever since I was little, I was afraid to make the wrong decisions; therefore, I had people make choices for me. I did this to a fault. So much that I simply did not know what I liked and what I did not. I desired to be like everyone else because I thought I wasn't good enough. I had an extreme fear of failing people in my life. Instead of making my own choices and being myself, I copied other people's characteristics.

"We need to make our desires, the Lord's desires."

Here are some examples. I never knew what entree to order at a restaurant, so I always had my parents order for me. When my friend signed up for gymnastics and dance class, so did I. When she quit, I followed right after her. I wanted to be a cheerleader because my best friend was. I listened to certain music or dressed in specific styles that my peers accepted. It eventually led me down the wrong path of underage drinking and promiscuity because my friends were living this lifestyle. I wanted to be accepted.

The strong experience of rejection in my middle school years carried with me into my adult life, so I was driven by the wrong desires. The incessant need to feel pretty and trendy, to be liked and admired, to be included and popular, and to not upset anyone gave me an impossibly unattainable view of life and people. Can you relate to this? As a Christian, we need to fight against these negative thought patterns daily. This is a prison to confine us, so we are not free to serve the one and true God.

We can get so consumed in the way people view us, we are not looking outward to the true needs of people in life around us. Jealousy, pride, and greed creep in and begin to destroy what the Lord is doing in us. We cannot let this happen. We need to make our desires the Lord's desires, and make sure that the only one we live to please is our Father in heaven and *NOT* people or the world.

After giving my life to Christ, I had to do a lot of soul-searching on this matter. I remember taking on the simple task of writing my name at the top of notebook paper and creating a list of all of the things that I, Nicole, liked and was interested in. It felt good to discover myself and meet the woman God created me to be.

If you, too, are a people pleaser and have lost who *YOU* are, I encourage you to write your name down and make a list as well! Ask God to help you discover the beautiful person He has created you to be. This simple act could be your significant breakthrough.

Things I like and are interested in...

Name: _____

1. _____

2. _____

3. _____

4. _____

5. _____

6. _____

7. _____

8. _____

9. _____

10. _____

11. _____

12. _____

13. _____

14. _____

Desire for Structure and Stability

Before I married Greg, I lived in the same house for 25 years. The only time I resided somewhere different was during my college years. Within the first four years of marriage, we moved four times! That is *NOT* in my nature ... *at ALL!* Greg thrives on change. I, on the other hand, enjoy structure and stability. Change makes me feel uneasy and nervous. I do not even like to move our furniture around because I'm such a creature of habit.

Some people are meant to be in one place for a very long time and for others, God has other plans. My journey with Christ has been dynamic, and God continues to teach and grow me through seasons of transition. As I wrote this book, God moved me from being a preschool teacher, to a job recruiter, to a day-to-day substitute teacher.

I love God's sense of humor in my current place of employment. For someone who dislikes change as much as me, I face it every day! As a substitute teacher, one is expected to walk into a different classroom daily and quickly absorb the teacher's plans and then execute lessons—all while keeping the children safe and happy. I love this job, but at the same time it makes me feel a little anxious and uncertain. Sometimes a complete nervous wreck!

The Lord teaches me about trust, flexibility, working with different personality types, and total reliance on Him. He reminds me of this truth as I live out Proverbs 3:5-6,

*"Trust in the Lord with all your heart, and
lean not on your own understanding. In all
your ways acknowledge him, and he shall
direct your paths."*

And the other verse I often rely on is Philippians 4:13,

*"I can do all things through Christ who
strengthens me."*

Through this phase of my life, the Lord is teaching me that although everything around me changes daily, God never does. He is my constant through it all!

Do you thrive on routine and consistency? This is not always bad, but in your relationship with God, it can be dangerous ... especially if you are not willing and able to follow where He leads. God might be telling you to change or give something up. Be careful that you don't serve yourself, rather than listen to and follow the Father's lead.

Here are two examples from scripture. One from the New Testament and the other from the Old Testament:

*"And as He walked by the Sea of Galilee, He
saw Simon and Andrew his brother casting a
net into the sea; for they were fishermen.
Then Jesus said to them, 'Follow Me, and I will
make you ... fishers of men.' They
immediately left their nets and followed
Him." (Mark 1:16-18)*

"Now the LORD had said to Abram:
'Get out of your country, from your family
and from your father's house, to a land that I
will show you. I will make you a great nation;
I will bless you and make your name great;
and you shall be a blessing. I will bless those
who bless you, and I will curse him who curses
you; and in you all the families of the earth
shall be blessed.'

So, Abram departed as the LORD had spoken to
him, and Lot went with him. And Abram was
seventy-five years old when he departed from
Haran." (Genesis 12:1-4)

I love how, in both cases, they went. Period. Simon and Andrew went immediately, and Abram went as the Lord told Him to. *Wow!*

How are you living in obedience to the Father? Are you so focused on your own routines that you do not see the Lord at work or desire to follow Him ... even when it requires change and discomfort?

If this is an obstacle in your life, pray that the Lord would help you to lay it down, live more flexibly, and walk in obedience to God.

Desire for Materialism:
Where or What is Your Treasure?

Over the years, the Lord has taught me valuable lessons on giving my materialistic desires over to Him. Admittedly, this is a lesson my stubborn heart has a difficult time learning, and God has taught me a lot of hard lessons about it. This seems to be a continual process, if I were to be honest.

At one time I was a full-time teacher, and Greg was a youth pastor. We were financially stable for a while before children. The moment I became pregnant with our oldest, Caleb, I resigned from teaching to be a stay-at-home mom. This was our choice and desire for our family. Throughout these years, my husband moved from being a youth pastor to an alternative education teacher; from a salesman to a seminary student; and finally from a youth pastor, again, to a pastor. *Whew!*

When I first resigned from teaching to stay home with our first baby, we did not have the security to keep up with our lifestyle, so we had to make some changes. We sold our dream home and downsized to something smaller, sold my little red sports car, rented a different home for a while, owned one very used van, and gave up on what we thought was the *"best of everything."*

This period of purging for us was extremely difficult, but good in so many ways. It gave a sense of freedom … to not be bound *by* or *to* "stuff." Was it difficult? You bet! Are the rewards the Lord gives greater than all of this? Absolutely!

*"For where your treasure is, there your heart
will be also." (Luke 12:34)*

Where or what is your treasure—with worldly possessions or with the Lord?

We all go through transitions and struggles. Setbacks and wrong turns. Is it easy? No. Does God always provide? I don't know about you, but we weren't always obedient, and our financial decisions didn't always honor God. But was God *always* faithful? YES. I praise our Lord Jesus because throughout every season of life, He is the *only* constant, shield, and provider. He took care of us even when we were not smart with our finances.

The Desire for Perfectionism

It was a normal day at home with my three beautiful children. They were the ages of seven, five, and one. The stages where toys were scattered everywhere! It did not matter that we had a play room designed just for the toys ... a designated place where the kids could actually play and make a mess. I mean, why would they really want to play in a playroom? Why go in there when we can have more room out where mommy is? This was the case in our home.

So, we had toddler toys scattered in about every single room, mounds of Star Wars® action figures far and wide, an assortment of Legos® planted like tiny grenades, along with baby dolls and Barbies® galore!

I remember feeling panic-stricken, trying to vacuum the stairs while commanding loudly for my three young children to help clean. I was so enraged over our messy home. My emotions escalated to a boiling point when the children began to taunt and fight with each other.

At that moment, I lost it! I became so angry that I banged the vacuum hose off of the rail, insisting that the kids clean up the horrible mess and stop fighting immediately. This cleaning frenzy had nothing to do with any deadline, like having guests over soon. It had everything to do with my unrealistic expectations and unwillingness to let go of having things done *my way*. I wanted things clean and orderly ... now!

There was so much ugliness in my heart at that moment, and it exploded on the little ones who I was entrusted with. My children looked at me wide-eyed and began to pick things up quickly. In that moment, I caught a glimpse of a woman I didn't recognize. How did I get to this point? I began to weep and feel frightened of the woman I was becoming. The woman my children were watching and learning from.

Once all three kids were snuggled in bed that night, my husband and I talked. You see, Greg is my best friend and my confidante. I have always been able to tell him how I feel, bounce ideas off of him, or ask for prayer when I so desperately needed it. That night we sat in the living room. I told him all about my erratic behavior in front of our precious children. I sat on the floor and wept with my head bowed in shame. I told him how I didn't want them to grow up and look back at what a freak their mother was. How she worried about cleaning the house and having things perfect.

I confessed to Greg something quite embarrassing ... how chaos and disorder made me feel sick. Yes, physically ill. I was concerned that I needed medication, secretly hoping this would be the solution. Greg is very calm and even keeled. He is wise and truthful. He balances me out in ways I could have never imagined. Did I mention he's truthful? I waited for a hug and for him to say, *"Yes, things were just too difficult, and I did need medical help."* And he'd assist me in making an appointment to get anxiety or depression medication. Well, this was not his reaction.

Greg looked right at me and kindly asked, *"How has your relationship with the Father been?"* *"What?"* I asked. I defended myself rather boldly! *"What do you mean 'How is my relationship with God?' I pray! I read my Bible! This isn't about God. It's about me and what I'm going through!"*

Ugh! I was so mad! That wasn't the response I wanted. After wallowing in self-pity for a while, making many poor excuses and firmly discussing my problems, I eventually became broken. I began to sob more and realized that my relationship with the Father did indeed need some work. A lot of work. It was distant, cold, unfruitful, inconsistent, rocky, and not where it should have been. I was distracted by life and busyness, not putting the Lord Jesus first.

That night, I came to the realization that I needed to repent and rededicate my life to the Lord ... and get down to business. Back to the basics. It was then that this became my new life verse:

*"Create in me a clean heart, Oh God, and
renew a steadfast spirit within me. Do not cast
me away from your presence and do not take
your Holy Spirit from me. Restore to me the
joy of your salvation and uphold me by Your
generous Spirit."* (Psalm 51:10-12)

I got down face first before the Father, repented, and asked for forgiveness and a fresh spirit to fall on me and to fill me. Praise God and thank you Lord Jesus for Your faithfulness, love, and forgiveness.

Please understand that I do strongly believe that God has given us doctors and medicine to help with ailments and in time of great need. My story, however, was different. After individually seeking and asking, I realized that I did not need medicine as a mask to cover a much deeper problem—my distance from Him. I needed to give up the need for perfectionism.

Perfectionism is an unrealistic goal. It is something that we put on ourselves. Not God. Perfectionism is a worldly attribute ... not Christ-like at all. We might try to defend the argument and say things like, *"This is just the way I am, and people have to accept it."* Or perhaps we might add, *"We are to always give our best to God and take care of the things He has given us."* Yes, I would agree with this second statement, but we must be very careful as to WHY we want things perfect.

Do we think God will love us less if we do not? Do we assume that our friends and family will think badly of us? Do we feel as if we're a failure if we don't achieve a certain goal?

Could it be our pride? These are some things to think and pray about. If perfectionism is an obstacle in your relationship with God or those you love, maybe it's time to repent.

Armor and a Used Van

The very used van we had for 10 years was having difficulty. This vehicle was a gracious gift from my mother-in-law. She was living with us at the time and said that it was ours. How wonderful to have a reliable vehicle for a family of five all those years! My husband's little black car was paid off. We had no car payments, and things were good. That is until one particular summer.

The van started to have all sorts of issues and was going to cost $5,000 to fix. We simply did not have that kind of extra money sitting around to put into a van that may not last. Not long after that, my husband's car began to act up. We were in a situation with no working vehicle at one point. Otherwise, when one worked, the other was out of commission.

We borrowed my mom's car more than I can ever remember. We even had dear friends lend us their van to take on vacation, so we would have ample room and a reliable vehicle. Praise God for the blessing of caring parents and good friends! God was present and provided.

This went on for almost six months. We did find another used van ... new to us and the kids. But that one ended up in the shop, too. We truly didn't understand why God allowed this to happen.

Despite all the car swapping and frustration, the Lord had worked in my heart through a Bible study about the Armor of God. The Lord prepared me for this difficult season by teaching me how to put on His armor daily to fight against the enemy of our souls.

You see, my husband is usually the calm one who doesn't easily frustrate, and I can be quite the opposite. Not this particular day! I remember looking my discouraged husband right in the eyes and confidently saying to him, as he dropped me off at work yet *again*,

> *"This world is not our home, and this stuff is not our own! It's going to be OK! Honestly, we have a healthy family, a roof over our heads, food to eat, and jobs to serve at. We do not need working vehicles to make us happy. We have all we need. We mustn't lose focus on what we are called to do!"*

The enemy of our soul is out to steal, kill, and destroy; I wasn't going to let him take our joy and destroy our focus. All of these possessions did not matter. We will not take them with us into eternity. Why do we hold onto these things so tightly? Why are they so important to us? Is it for prideful reasons? To be recognized? To be like everyone else? To feel significant? To fit in? To please our children? These are all pressures of the world, but the scriptures call us to be different.

Envision your heart as a puzzle made up of many separate pieces—perhaps even some that are broken and shattered. Either way, now that you've given Christ your heart, give back some things you've tried to take charge of ... your desires being one of them.

What yearnings gnaw at your heart? To find the right spouse? To go on a missions trip? To be a stay-at-home mom? To have expensive things? To always be right? To end a rocky marriage? To please everyone? To be financially stable? To adopt a child? To be a perfectionist? To always be the best? To be prettier and always noticed?

Our Desires Become His Desires

Stop right now and confess these areas where you fight to let go. Give them to God. Repent of the need to control these desires of your life. Whether they are for good or a byproduct of evil, give them all back because you are not your own. You've been bought by the blood of Christ, and you need to honor God by giving Him your all. Let Jesus take over and bring peace and healing.

When God's desires become our desires, He changes us. God's way is best, and His timing is perfect—even when we do not understand. Don't try to figure it out because most times it won't make any sense to you. Psalm 37:4 states,

"Delight yourself also in the LORD,
And He shall give you the desires of your
heart."

I know when I was young in the faith, I thought it meant if I believed in God, He would give me whatever I wanted. Secretly, I think a lot of us interpret this scripture that way. It wasn't until recently that the Lord helped me fully understand what this verse means.

"*Delight yourself in the Lord.*" In English, _delight_ means "*extreme satisfaction.*" In Hebrew, _delight_ has several meanings: *chaphets* or "*to bend towards*" and anag "*to be soft and delicate.*" The root of <u>anag</u> is interesting because it means "*pliable.*"

What does this mean to us? If we bend towards God and take pleasure in Him and all His goodness, we grow closer to Him. In this soft moldable state, we become more like Him. When we become more like God, our desires and passions change to be more like His. So, the yearnings of our hearts are no longer our selfish worldly cravings, but God's desires for us. When we walk in obedience to God, He does bless us for that obedience.

Like Deuteronomy 11:27 says,

> God will give "the blessing, if you obey the
> commandments of the LORD your God that I
> am giving you today."

When you seek Him with all your heart and immerse yourself in the Word, prayer, and the body of Christ, your desires will become His desires, and you will be used for purposes greater than you could have ever imagined.

Below, write the desires you need to give over to God.
Pray and ask Him to take them and help you to discern which are good and which are not of Him. Ask Him to make His desires your desires. May you feel His peace as you surrender.

_____

_____

_____

_____

_____

_____

_____

_____

_____

_____

_____

_____

_____

_____

_____

_____

_____

_____

_____

_____

_____

_____

_____

_____

Chapter 4
The Pieces of My Reputation

Shortly after having the abortion and giving my life to Christ, I attended a University Christian Fellowship meeting at school. That evening, the guest speaker was from the nearby Women's Care Center. I truly believe that she was sent there by God just for me. I was growing in my faith but was so full of guilt, shame, and unforgiveness.

I vaguely remember what she spoke about that evening. But all I knew was, after hearing this gentle woman's message of hope, I had to seek her out the next day. Subsequently, she became my counselor and helped me work through the shame and guilt I felt for so long. It brought me peace to talk openly about what I experienced through and after the abortion, including Post Traumatic Stress Disorder. During our first session, she taught me something that I will never forget:

> I learned that when we go through circumstances
> that cause us deep hurt and pain, we must
> deal with them. A traumatic experience is

47

like a flesh wound. When we get a deep lesion and do not treat it properly and immediately, it then gets infected and sometimes hurts worse and takes longer to heal. It usually develops into a larger problem that aches even more.

She said that we must treat this wound with the proper care. We must give our attention to it and break it open. This is messy and difficult, but the wound must be exposed and cleaned out the right way so it will heal properly. There may be a scar, which is always a reminder, but it is no longer painful.

It's the same with a hurtful life experience. We must not simply ignore the discomfort, or it will only get worse and create more complications and added despair. This all made complete sense to me as I began my slow and arduous journey of freedom and total healing.

So, what does this have to do with reputation? Personally, I hid my abortion and attempted suicide because I was utterly disappointed in myself for making an unspeakable decision that defied God and hurt others. Not to mention, I was terribly ashamed of what people would think of me, fearful they would judge me by what I did and the choices I'd made. You may have something you're hiding deep in your soul. Something you don't talk about. What if *"they,"* too, think you are less of a person because of your past struggles?

Trading in Our Reputations

Let's dig in a little deeper. Do reputations really matter to God? The word <u>reputation</u> means *"the overall quality or character as seen or judged by people in general."* A character as *SEEN* or *JUDGED* by whom? *PEOPLE.* So, we worry and fret about what people think of us. I've mentioned my intense struggle with living as a people pleaser my whole life.

Even after two decades of being a Christ follower, I still fight it every day. I have always been concerned about what other people think of my parenting skills, the way I look, or what I'm wearing. What if *"they"* do not like the way I respond or if I do something incorrectly? What if I upset *"them"* or *"they"* do not like me? What will *"they"* think of our home, or what if I am not a good pastor's wife and don't meet *"their"* expectations? Who are *"they,"* anyway? Can we even answer that question?

In reality, isn't it quite arrogant to think that people think so highly of us? That they spend all their time only thinking of us? It sounds absolutely ridiculous, doesn't it? Then why do we as human beings place such value on our reputations? Do they really matter? Or more importantly, are they important to God?

I think God wants us to trade in our reputations. That's right. Leave our reputations and the worries of what others think of us at the foot of the cross, and concern ourselves with *character*—our mental and moral qualities God-breathed into each of us. He desires our life choices to be made in such a way that are pleasing to Him and in line with His truth.

Yes, our spiritual character holds the greatest significance; our *"worldly reputations"* do not. The material things of this world—like personal achievements and social status—should not matter. They do not make an eternal impact, and we can't take them with us into the next life; this includes our physical bodies and the opinions of other people we tend to hold so high.

It is sin to hold onto this and think that we have it all together—that there is something wrong with us when we do not. We must stop being concerned and consumed with what others think of us and be more focused on Jesus, His thoughts, and His ways.

Sure, it feels risky, as believers, to share our past or our faith in general, out of fear

"I think God wants us to trade in our reputations. That's right. Leave our reputation and worry of what others think of us at the foot of the cross, and concern ourselves with character—our mental and moral qualities Goa-breathed into each of us."

of affecting our reputations in some way. Yes, some people could pass judgement on us. But to open ourselves up, become vulnerable, and share all that the Lord has done ... for His glory and perhaps to save a soul? That takes Godly character. You see, there are other people who need to hear the wondrous work of God in us *(in all its messiness)* to help themselves heal. Unfolding my *dark, ugly secret* was something that could have very easily altered the view my family, friends, and children had of me.

When I first submitted to God and began to write my story, I didn't have any intention of revealing my abortion. I remember specifically being on a walk, and while standing in the field behind my house, God told me otherwise. Through much prayer and reflection, He revealed that this was something I was indeed called to do. In my human *"Nicole attitude,"* I would much rather have kept it to myself. I could still share other parts of my life and glorify the Lord without sharing THAT! Surely NOT that, God. His voice was clear: *"Nicole, you have to share this. Your brokenness is what led you to me. This huge part matters."*

I remember falling to my knees in utter surrender that day. I accepted and embraced the fact that this was something I was called to do, and that God would be with me. I didn't need to worry about people's opinions.

We do most certainly need to be concerned about being obedient to God and His ways. What is God calling you to share, and who does He want you to share with? Ask God for His wisdom and strength to open up about your life. Ask Him to help you let go of the tight grip you have on your reputation and give you wisdom to live with character.

Let Go of the Past Reputation: Let There Be Healing and Freedom

When you look at your own life and relationship with the Father, you may not have had a huge conversion experience like the drug dealer down the street, the Apostle Paul, or even me. But when you are a child of God ... you have a story. He died for your sins. He loves you and is full of grace.

If you never fell away from God ... praise Him! That is the best testimony ever! To walk with God your entire life is an amazing witness of His protection and faithfulness. I pray for a strong, steadfast, and unshakable faith for my own children.

If you've had an abortion or have suffered some other dark sin or traumatic circumstance that is too difficult to bear, please do *three* things for me.

1. Know that you are forgiven! When you ask God for forgiveness ... it's done. He doesn't need to be reminded over and over because His Word says He forgives your sins and throws them away. Once you ask, you are forgiven. The enemy of our souls is the one who piles on heaps of guilt, shame, and constant reminders. God's truth brings freedom from the enemy's stinking thinking and builds character.

*"For I will be merciful to their
unrighteousness, and their sins and their
lawless deeds I will remember no more."
(Hebrews 8:12)*

*"If we confess our sins, he is faithful and just
to forgive us our sins and to cleanse us from
all unrighteousness."
(1 John 1:9)*

*"Though your sins are like scarlet, they shall
be white as snow; though they are red like
crimson, they shall be as wool."
(Isaiah 1:18)*

*"For God so loved the world that He gave His
only begotten son, that whoever believes in
Him should not perish but have everlasting
life." (John 3:16)*

2. Please get help. Talk to someone. We are not meant to go through trials alone. You can seek out a trusted Christian friend or a Godly Counselor. They won't judge you. Do not hold it inside. It will destroy you.

3. Know that you are worthy of His love and worthy to be used for Kingdom purposes. Your so-called reputation doesn't matter, but your obedience does. The Bible is full of imperfect individuals that He gave His power, strength, wisdom, and guidance to, in order to be used for Him and by Him. You are worthy! It gives me comfort to know that God uses us in spite of ourselves. He uses the imperfect to assist the Perfect *(God)* to fulfill His purposes and plans!

REFLECT on the three things I asked of you.

Write down the step you are at...is it 1, 2, or 3?

Step: _____. Ask God to intervene and help you to heal.

Your past does not define you. Who you are in Christ defines you:

- *You are a child of the King.*
- *You are forgiven and set free.*
- *You are worthy.*
- *You are loved.*
- *You are chosen.*
- *You are useful.*

Lay these pieces down and let the peace of Christ fill your heart and life.

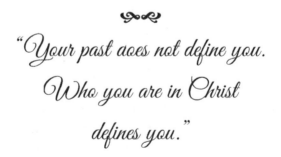

"Your past does not define you. Who you are in Christ defines you."

Chapter 5
The Pieces of Control: A Two-Way Street

The older I get, the more frightened I am of heights. This fear has always been a part of me, but more so now than ever. Although I enjoy the thrill of a large roller coaster, the anticipation makes me sick. As I wait in line and slowly approach the ride, my stomach churns, my heart beats, my nerves become jittery, and I'm just plain terrified!

My husband and friends think I'm a bit loony as I pray to Jesus while I strap myself in and hold on tight as we gradually climb to the pinnacle of the hill. I close my eyes and panic. I think I'm going to die! Truly!

I feel the same way about flying in an airplane. I've only traveled two times by plane in my life. Both times I was not happy ... at all! Frankly, the thought of it now terrifies me. I have nightmares of falling and crashing. I would so much rather drive wherever we need to go, including the almost two-day trek to Disney World my family took a few years ago.

I didn't mind one bit. Our five-year-old got carsick all over everything in the van, and I still did not care.

Why, you may ask, am I afraid of roller coasters and of flying in an air plane? *Because I am not the one in control.* These activities are 100 percent out of my hands. I am not the one conducting, operating, or directing anything. It's all about trust. It's all about faith. When I am not the one in control of something, it makes me nervous. Why do we have such a need for control? Why does being in charge help us to feel safe and stable?

Some find comfort in control, but this can be very dangerous when it comes to faith. If you gave your heart to Jesus, then *that is* trust and faith. So, what happens when you prefer to be in the driver's seat, like me? We all can say in words that we trust the Lord with our lives, marriages, children, jobs, finances, health, homes, etc. ... but we don't always show it with our actions.

The Need to Control Took Over Me

I was 23 years old and fresh out of college with a degree in elementary and special education. My high school offered me a long-term substitute teaching position in the Learning Support class, teaching students with learning disabilities.

It was strange to work alongside some of my past teachers, all of whom I looked up to and respected. So, as a perfectionist and a highly anxious young woman, I took this job extremely seriously. I was new, and there was so much to learn and understand.

My students were only a few years younger than me, and many of them had emotional disorders in addition to learning disabilities. I poured my heart and soul into this position, spending endless hours each day preparing for my student's individual needs and collaborating with the other teachers. I was new at all of this and stretched myself each step of the way.

The summer before I moved into this teaching position, I innocently delved into a vigorous eating plan and exercise routine. I have always been somewhat athletic and active. Although never really overweight, you could say I was *"healthy."* I previously worked with some women who were dieting and very much into fitness and wellness. Don't get me wrong, I think it is important to be healthy. It's vital to take care, love, and attend to our bodies the best we can. We certainly honor God by taking care of what He has given us.

But there I was, in my early 20s with a new job, working hard to impress my co-workers, meet my students' needs, and maintain this so-called diet and exercise "plan." A plan I never researched or consulted a trainer or dietician about before I started. A strategy I made up myself.

As I became more and more dedicated to my job, my insecurities grew and my eating and exercising became more and more rigid. I set boundaries and goals for myself that could not be bent or changed one bit. These goals were very unreasonable and unrealistic. The more I felt overwhelmed in my career or personal life, the firmer and stricter I became in my health. I felt in control. I had to be in command of something, and this made me feel safe. Or, so I thought.

As I slowly put this eating and exercise regime ahead of everything in my life ... I moved Jesus, my Savior, off to the side. I made Him second best as dieting became my god. I *thought* I was in charge, but in reality, this obsession was in charge of me. I allowed it to consume me in such a way that I lived in fear. You see, I only allowed myself to eat a certain number of calories (without ever giving myself any grace), with very limited carbs. And I had to power walk every single day. *EVERY. SINGLE. DAY.*

When I say this, I mean no matter what time ... midnight, 2 AM, immediately after work. No matter the weather ... rain, sleet, blizzard conditions, or 100-degree weather. No matter what other plans I may have had ... family occasions, church activities, or time with friends ... *every single day.*

I felt that if I did not get my power-walk in, then I would completely fall apart and come undone. I somehow thought I would gain 10 pounds back by not walking for one day. I felt helpless and like a failure and quickly plunged into a pattern of only eating certain foods. I was terrified of ALL other foods except the "*safe*" foods on my plan.

I didn't know how to make wise decisions or choose healthy alternative meals while out with friends and family. As a result, I isolated myself from people as much as I could— even my family, Greg, and our friends. It seemed easier to be alone. No pressure. No difficult questions to answer. It was dreadful to go to events and social gatherings because I didn't know what food they would serve. I simply couldn't deal with the pressure of making those decisions.

I dropped weight fast and began to get attention from people. They said I looked good, but inside my heart was full of sadness, loneliness, lethargy, and hunger. I began to look like a skeleton and became fearful to gain weight. The unrealistic expectations of myself gave me a warped view of my body. I was self-consumed. Something innocent and good turned into an addiction. Something I thought I had a grasp on, slowly took hold of me ... *mind, body, and spirit.*

Relationships in my life began to suffer—with my parents, my sister, my friends, and yes, with Greg. They could all see me slipping away, becoming a different person who was only focused on herself and all her personal issues.

You see, if we are not aware and do not give up total control to Jesus, it's way too easy to let other things creep in and become more important than Him. We can choose to do something that is not bad at all, like eating healthy and exercising. However, if not careful, we subtly become consumed and it becomes our *all*. It takes over our mind, heart, every movement, moment, thought, and action.

It may become the only topic of conversation with everyone and anyone we meet. Rationalization could call it a passion. However, God is a jealous God. He makes this clear in Exodus 34:14,

> *"For you shall worship no other god, for the*
> LORD, *whose name is Jealous, is a jealous*
> *God."*

When we put anything on the throne in place of our Savior, we set ourselves up for utter failure. We find ourselves in the middle of idolatry.

I allowed this to happen to me; my quest for *"healthy"* living turned into an eating disorder. You see, my idol of food and exercise turned into anorexia and then to bulimia. I taught a rigorous schedule all day at school, then after work I would give in to temptation and purchase large amounts of food. I would consume everything quickly to the point of sickness, drive to a park or isolated location, and purge it all. Then I would punish myself by spending hours over-exercising to make up for what I had done. I would cry and become a total wreck. It felt so wrong, and I would ask the Lord to help and forgive me for this disgusting and embarrassing sin. Ironically, in my need to keep control, I completely lost control.

I finally realized my need for help when none of my clothes fit me. I stopped getting my menstrual cycle; I was cold, hungry, and depressed all the time. Greg and I took a break from dating because I could not handle my own life, let alone a relationship. My parents confronted me and told me that I was on a very dangerous path that could lead to death. That was my wake-up call.

Since I didn't want to lose my life this young, I agreed to see a counselor. I was not in control of my eating, or my life, for that matter. In fact, I made a big mess of things. I was in the middle of a sickness, and I wanted to get better. I wanted to be me again. The Nicole everyone knew. Recognizing my need for help was the first step.

I found a Christian counselor who helped me break my cycle of repetitive sin and addiction as well as the negative patterns of thinking. During one of my counseling sessions, he said to me, *"Nicole, you must stop the cycle. No matter what. When you recognize you are in the middle of an addictive behavior, you must call on God and stop it!"*

I despised the fact that large amounts of food were in me, but I took my counselor's advice to heart and started to find strength in Christ to halt my erratic behavior. Healing wasn't easy. It was a fight. It was hard work. There were many failures, but God helped me gain victory over this sin issue in my life. Because that is what it was ... *sin.* I allowed the need for control—my fixation with eating and exercising— to consume and take me over ... *it was sin.*

Through prayer, perseverance, and support, I did eventually overcome. Our gracious God helped me to have the strength and wisdom to be 100 percent healed from this mental and physical prison. It took all I had to stop the downward spiral of sin by choosing *not* to purge all the food I consumed in my binges, but I started to find strength in Christ.

By choosing to stop the vicious cycle, the enemy became powerless, losing his impact on me. Only Christ, my Savior, had this kind of influence and authority. I finally began to acknowledge God's power and call on Him for help. I did not ask the Father to magically take it all away. It doesn't always work that way. I called on Jesus to give me the desire to fight the battle each day because ...

"I can do all things through Christ who strengthens me." (Philippians 4:13)

It took many years of counseling, praying, and seeking God and His truth to completely set me free from this stronghold in my life. This can be true for you, too. What is it that you want to control? Your marriage? Your children? How people view you? Your bank account? Your job? Your household? Your ministry? Your health? What is it that you think you can do better than God? What takes priority over Him?

Take some time to pray and repent. If you need to ask a trusted friend or prayer partner for help ... *this is the time.* The things you want to control *can* become an addiction. They can and will take over and become an infection. Think about going to work or to a public place, and someone is sick. If you touch them or are exposed to the germ, it gets on you and, in your body, *then it spreads.* If you don't treat it and take the right medicine, the sickness consumes your body.

The same thing happens with sin, especially with addictive behaviors or the need to control. If we dabble in it, even a little, it can quickly and subtly take over. Then we find ourselves completely infected. We think *we* know what is best in our lives, and before long, *BOOM* ... we're in the middle of a mess ... *a sickness.*

Our human need for control is rooted in pride, which leads to many other problems and addictive behaviors such as eating disorders, alcoholism, drugs, sexual addictions, materialism, and perfectionism, to name a few.

But there are situations in life we were either born into or that basically just happened to us. We don't have any influence over these circumstances, and they become too much to bear. We can let these tragedies or problems devastate our lives.

Perhaps you were brought into the world with a disability or sickness, born into an abusive or impoverished home life, suffer with chronic pain, mourn the death of a child or spouse, experience depression or anxiety, or were victimized. If we let them, these issues can become such a heavy burden—a darkness that we allow to take control—they result in bitterness that cannot be shaken.

We allow our negative circumstances to steal our joy and purpose for living. They consume our every thought like a toxic poison. Even though we have no control over much of these situations of life, we cannot let them control us. Please know this attitude is not of Christ.

Whether self-inflicted or otherwise, these problems are so very emotionally exhausting and painful. If we don't accept and properly address them, they quickly become like the infection I just mentioned.

In 2 Corinthians 10:5, Paul wrote:

*"... We demolish arguments and every
pretension that sets itself up against the
knowledge of God, and we take captive every
thought to make it obedient to Christ ..."*

This means we are not to daydream and let our thoughts wander. When we do this, we start believing the stories in our minds or what people dictate to us, rather than what's real. This takes us down a dark path. A course we have no business taking. That's where the two-way street comes in.

The Two-Way Street: Control Is a Choice

When I am upset with someone or experience an extremely difficult situation, I tend to replay it in my mind over and over and over. But I do my best to immediately quote God's truth and refocus my attention. This is one of the verses I'll say out loud:

> *"Set your minds on things above, not on*
> *earthly things. For you died, and your life is*
> *now hidden with Christ in God."*
> *(Colossians 3:2-3)*

I encourage you to do the same when you find yourself in a similar situation. Think of it this way: our thoughts are like a GPS. How many times have you typed in your destination and followed the route to get there? When you make a wrong turn, what does it say? *"Reroute!" "Reroute!"* It is much the same with our perceptions. We should be focused on Jesus. He *IS* our destination.

However, when we let our thoughts make a wrong turn and travel down another path, we need to say, "REROUTE!" We must redirect our thoughts to the Lord Jesus, or we will get lost! You are likely thinking this is easier said than done. And you're right. It's not easy, even as a Christian. It's a choice, perhaps even the hardest decision you'll make every day.

I have always struggled deeply with my thought life. Greg would know immediately when I was having a difficult time because he would say, *"Where are you, Nicole? You are not here right now."* My thoughts were dark, and I slipped into a fantasy, which led to depression. I would obsess about my body shape or appearance, comparing myself to other women. I would constantly replay a conversation in my mind, wondering if a specific friend or family member was angry at me by the way they looked at me at work or church. I would fantasize about other people's homes and wondered why we did not have all the nice things the family down the street had.

I would also think about my students and if I was doing my absolute best to educate them. Oh, and what about worrying about my children and if they had friends at school. And I'd dwell on the fact that I don't measure up as the perfect pastor's wife. Woe is me! This is all a trap of the enemy—sin.

When our thoughts fixate on ourselves and our problems, we cannot see those in need around us because we're so inwardly consumed. This toxic behavior keeps us from the Lord and all He has for us. There is a barrier around us, and we allowed it to be built. It's an obstacle between us and the Father who loves us so very much. The One who died for us. The One who says,

> *"I have called you by your name; you are mine." (Isaiah 43:1)*

We must acknowledge this stronghold and tear it down. You see, the enemy cannot steal our salvation, but he sure can mess things up and make us feel powerless or useless. We feel insignificant, unimportant, and wonder how God could ever use us when we are such a hot mess. The good news is that God can and will deliver us if we choose His way over our own stubborn ways! He can heal and strengthen us. He can set us free and use us in mighty ways to minister in His name ... all for His glory! We must be awake, alert, and on our guard at all times! Like it says in 1 Peter 5:8-10:

> *"Be alert and of sober mind. Your enemy the devil prowls around like a roaring lion looking for someone to devour. Resist him, standing firm in the faith, because you know that the family of believers throughout the world is undergoing the same kind of sufferings. And the God of all grace, who called you to his eternal glory in Christ, after you have suffered a little while, will himself restore you and make you strong, firm and steadfast."*

"After you have suffered a little while." I love that! Even though it may seem like forever, we are on this earth for such a short time. The amount of time we suffer on this earth is just a little while in comparison to eternity. So, after we suffer *a little while,* He will restore us and make us strong. Can I hear an Amen?

I have known too many women who have suffered with aching hearts for too long, so many kind and caring daughters of the King who are filled with grief and bitterness instead of joy and peace. Sorrows have taken over and suffocated the thoughts of these precious lives. However, it's also a choice to hold on to the past and not let go. They constantly look back instead of to the present. They miss out on the *"now"* because they think about what could have been or are still so wounded and hurt, they simply cannot move on.

"We can choose to take the road of defeat, or we can choose to walk in victory through Christ."

This bondage has robbed them of years of freedom that comes with knowing Christ. Jesus does not want this for us. The enemy of our souls wants us to be so consumed in our problems that we are not awake and aware of what God is doing in, through, and around us.

We need to recognize these sad and bitter thoughts and ask the Lord to forgive us, heal us, and take them away. To lay them at the foot of the cross once and for all. We *can* choose joy, and we *can* choose to overcome. It is important to grieve properly and deal with our hurts and emotions, but then we must move on and see outside ourselves.

There is a whole world of hurt, my friend. But it is a two-way street. We can choose to take the road of defeat, or we can choose to walk in victory through Christ.

A verse I love and find great satisfaction and relief in is in 2 Corinthians 1:3-4.

> *"Praise be to the God and Father of our Lord Jesus Christ, the Father of compassion and the God of all comfort, who comforts us in all our troubles, so that we can comfort those in any trouble with the comfort we ourselves receive from God."*

Yes, He can and will use our hurts and difficult situations to help others in need.

Turning Tragedy into Triumph

She was my childhood best friend. We spent many summer days together for sleepovers, frolicking down by the river, singing songs, playing dress-up, cheerleading, playing with Barbie dolls, and simply being silly. We remained friends throughout high school but drifted apart during college.

In 2012 something tragic happened to her and her family. Happily married with two precious little girls, she and her parents took a family vacation to Florida. During their time away, her oldest daughter, who was only 8 years old at the time, was tragically killed in a boating accident.

My heart was shocked and broken for her. Having little ones of my own, I grieved for her as I digested such horrific news. Our family was leaving for a church retreat for the weekend, so we could not attend the funeral. I felt helpless.

I couldn't fathom the agony, anger, confusion, distress, emptiness, and pain my friend felt. Such deep sorrow. How could one overcome and move on? How could one ever really be the same? I never really spoke to my friend in detail about these events, but I do know what I observe. I see a woman who still has another daughter to live and care for and who chooses to move forward. She isn't paralyzed by grief or depression. I am not saying that there are never sleepless nights of deep hurt or anguish, but her family chooses to take the next step and live life. And guess what? This family chooses to bring something good and positive out of their horrific situation.

They created a scholarship program in their sweet daughter's name to bless graduating seniors in their home school district. My friend wrote a book to encourage grieving siblings. She maintains a blog and Facebook page to keep her daughter's memory alive and to encourage others who are hurting. She chooses to not let bitterness take root and consume her life. I see a woman who lives out 2 Corinthians 1:4, choosing to let God help and comfort others with the same comfort He gave her.

Control *is* a two-way street, friend. You can choose to control every aspect of your life and risk serious problems like addiction, compulsive action, or a thought process that is not Christ-like or healthy. Further, you can choose to let tragedies and devastation control you to a point of helpless bitterness, which consumes every area of your life like a toxic poison. And when you allow difficulties to overtake you, joy, peace, or freedom in Christ is not possible. You are sick. However, you can *choose* to break free of these chains!

I know it's easy to forget how much power you have in the name of Jesus. He knows your every need and all your deep hurts. He has been there. Please don't think for one minute that He doesn't care. He cares so much—more than we could ever understand. Please, please do not take one more step in the bondage of control. It is exhausting and ineffective. It is impossible.

Choose to break-free from your need for control. Choose to give it to Christ. Let go, and let Christ have complete dominion over your life, thoughts, and actions. Let Him be the Lord of all.

Here are some steps to start:

- ✎ **Admit** your need for control and your desire to be free.

- ✎ **Confess** this stronghold as sin, laying it all down at the feet of Jesus *daily.*

- ✎ **Think** about what step you should take to stop the cycle of your sin, with God as your strength. If needed, seek out a professional to help you sort it out.

Friend, Jesus is waiting for you.

> *"Come to Me, all you who labor and are heavy*
> *laden, and I will give you rest."*
> *(Matthew 11:28)*

Please know how much He loves and values you. He knows best. Even if it is scary to surrender control, remember you were never really in charge to begin with.

When there is a two-way street, you have a choice. I pray you choose a better way—victory in Christ! All the glory goes to our Heavenly Father; He has already won the battle!

> *"Now the Lord is Spirit and where the Spirit of*
> *the Lord is, there is freedom."*
> *(2 Corinthians 3:17)*

> *"Be anxious for nothing, but in everything by*
> *prayer and supplication, with thanksgiving,*
> *let your requests be made known to God; and*
> *the peace of God, which surpasses all*
> *understanding, will guard your hearts and*
> *minds through Christ Jesus."*
> *(Philippians 4:6-7)*

❧

"I pray you choose a better way –
Victory in Christ!"

Chapter 6
The Pieces of My Schedule

As I sit here and begin to type this chapter, I sit in a very old castle-like building. The structure smells of antique furniture, maintains beautiful hardwood floors, and contains three different staircases just to reach the second level. It is built of gorgeous gray stone and has three rather long wings filled with cozy guest rooms. The prayer tower is way up at the pinnacle of the building. Two sets of staircases must be climbed to reach it.

As for my room, well, it is unbelievable. Gorgeous and undeserved. I have a lovely Victorian queen-sized bed, four large open windows that are positioned above another window, boasting a beautiful view of the lush forest and hills. A stately looking fireplace, a lovely private bathroom, and a large open desk made of dark wood, rounds out the exquisite ambiance. At the desk I sit with my Bible, keyboard, and cup of hot coffee. I feel so blessed to be here. My family calls this Holy place *"The Castle,"* but its real name is Life Ministries. At one time it was owned by the wealthiest people in Franklin, Pennsylvania. It was sold and used as a convent, but is now utilized as a Christian prayer and retreat center. Greg and I have been here countless times with various youth groups for spirit-filled adventurous getaways. This time it's different; it's quiet and peaceful because I am by myself.

You see, God called me to write nearly 15 years ago. I knew God spoke this over my life, but I was not yet prepared. And it wasn't until a month prior to this retreat that God spoke very clearly: *"Now Nicole. Go and be alone with Me. Be still."*

This is really out of my character. My life, just like yours, is full of all kinds of obligations. Prior to coming here to Life Ministries, I had wrapped up our pre-school year with a grand graduation, an exciting school picnic, and an exhausting day of packing up my classroom. My friend and I were prepping for our Vacation Bible School kick-off as well.

As I write, it's also Memorial Day weekend, and our church family is passing out hot dogs and goodies to the community. I am preparing to train for and begin a new summer job. Oh, did I mention that my husband's birthday is this weekend on top of running to baseball games, baton twirling lessons, and scouting? But in the midst, God called me to come away. The timing seemed incredibly crazy, but my husband also said something crazier to me, *"There is no better time than this."*

Help! I'm So Busy and Crazy; How Do I Fit It All in?

Busy-ness is a very real and growing epidemic, and I am in no way exempt. Just a few weeks ago, my schedule was so jam packed, I pulled in the driveway to unload groceries and forgot to shut off my van! It not only ran out of gas, but the battery died as well. What a delightful surprise I had the next morning when I tried to leave for work. A lot of good the hurry did me. What does Jesus have to say about all of this busy-ness? What does He think when we hysterically run around from one thing to the next? When we are so busy that we don't think clearly? It sometimes feels like we are hamsters running on a wheel and never get anywhere.

We say we really do love Jesus as our Savior, BUT we have work, sports activities, grocery shopping, laundry, housework, homework, gardening, vacation, concerts, and projects. Our actions say we don't have enough time for Jesus. Period. It's no wonder we can't find peace.

It reminds me of a text I received from my dear cousin, Connie. She said she wanted to live with *"kingdom goals"* in mind, not *"Connie goals."*

"Connie goals are when I waste time playing games on my phone and not reading my Bible or seeking the Lord more," she explained to me. I love that! I don't know about you, but I sure want to live for kingdom goals and not the rat race! With this in mind, let's take a closer look at the pieces of our schedule through the lens of God's kingdom.

I'm Too Busy to Rest

God makes it clear that we are to rest. After He created the world and everything in it, He rested on the seventh day. We are to live by His example and take a Sabbath— to be still and listen for His voice. Having places to go and people to see is a part of life, and certainly not all our activities are inherently *"bad."* However, we tend to ridiculously overdo it, then collapse out of pure exhaustion. In that respect we don't truly rest; we become lazy—too tired and unwilling to move or use our energy for anything productive.

To find true rest, you must first give your schedule to God. Why? Because your life is not your own; you gave your all to Him when you asked Him to be Lord of your life. Your family calendar is included in this *"all"* because it is time God gave you. It is precious and limited. What a smart tactic of the enemy ... to keep you so busy and distracted that you don't have time for what is most important ... time with your Savior.

Are You a Slave to Your Schedule or Free to Obey?

In our family, Greg and I try our hardest to put God ahead of our schedule. We are human and fail at this, many times over. Still, obedience is an important priority for our family, as we encourage each other to choose God's way over our own.

It's not really a second thought. He is the Lord of our individual lives and our family's life. It takes work, especially when it comes to our family calendar. On our local Christian radio station one day, they posed a question about busy schedules ... particularly related to sports. The question was something like,

> "Is it wrong to have our children's activities take over our lives, especially if they take us away from church on Sunday? Or is it OK because the times have changed, and expectations are different with sports and activities in today's world?"

This is a very sensitive issue for my husband and me, and we firmly stand in agreement. If we go to God's Word for some help, I think the answer is very clear,

> *"For the Lord your God is a consuming fire, a jealous God." (Deuteronomy 4:23)*

> *"But seek first the Kingdom of God and His righteousness, and all these things shall be added to you." (Matthew 6:33)*

> *"No one can serve two masters; for either he will hate the one and love the other, or else he will be loyal to the one and despise the other. You cannot serve God and riches." (Matthew 6:24)*

Fill in the blank for yourself:

You cannot serve God and _____.

Have we made our children's activities *(or ours, for that matter)* more important than God? Have we built up idols by making sports or activities our God? Have we been living in the flesh and serving another master other than the Lord? If God and His Word never change, why do we think we can alter it in such a way that it's fine to squeeze God in where it's convenient? How can we feel that He is alright with this?

If multiple family activities conflict in everyday life, how do we choose? We choose the Lord first. All it takes is a simple prayer like, *"Lord, what would you have us do?"*

Greg and I are strongly against flippantly skipping church because of a sporting event or extracurricular activity. But we also know if we earnestly seek Him, Jesus may call us to a church event to join with our brothers and sisters in service, or God could call us to another activity. He can certainly use us in some way in a unique location. Perhaps somebody needs to feel the love of Christ who is not at church.

It is *not often* that we skip church because of other life events. You see, my husband worked with youth for the majority of his ministry. He was a youth pastor before we were married, and I had the privilege of serving the Lord alongside him. We sadly witnessed teens eliminating youth group, retreats, opportunities to serve, and Sunday morning worship due to sports or jobs. We understand commitment and responsibility, but to what or whom do we serve when we cut

out church altogether? In Ecclesiastes, King Solomon even
states,

> *"Utterly meaningless!*
> *Everything is meaningless. What do people*
> *gain from all their labors at which they toil*
> *under the sun? Generations come and*
> *generations go, but the earth remains*
> *forever." (1:2-4)*

Activities are fun and an important part of all our lives,
however, what are they in light of eternity?

Ask God First

Our oldest son Caleb completed his first year of middle school
and received an award for high honors. Greg and I couldn't
have been more pleased when we heard the news. Of course,
13-year-old boys don't communicate or bring home important
information from school in a timely manner. And we found
that the awards ceremony was three days away!

Not only was it the week of pre-school graduation
where I taught, but a singing group was scheduled to perform
at our church that same night. Yes, two events on the same
night. *Of course.*

As the pastor's wife, I truly wanted to support my
husband as he hosted this special evening, which had been on
our calendar for months. And as much as I desired to see this
singing group in action, I couldn't *"punish"* our child for

receiving high honors at school by not attending his special night. I felt the Lord nudge me to go with Caleb, while Greg stayed back at the church.

Since we paused to give our schedule to God, He was so good as to allow my son and me to greet all the talented singers as they arrived and even had time to watch the first part of the concert. We made it in plenty of time for the awards ceremony. Boy, was I glad I went! Not only was I there to show love, encouragement, and support to our son, but God had something special in store. Something I needed, especially as I planned to begin my writing journey the very next day.

When we arrived at the program, my son ran off with his friends. There in the lobby was my friend and her husband, along with a former co-worker. The four of us sat in the auditorium together and had a chance to chat and catch up. My friend, who I had not seen in quite a few years, leaned over to me and said, *"Nicole, there is something I've been meaning to tell you for some time now, but I didn't know how."*

I had a concerned look on my face, which she saw right through. *"It's nothing bad! I just felt awkward calling and didn't know how to tell you,"* she added.

My friend revealed that while at church, her teen daughter was asked to reflect upon and write about the time that she gave her life to Jesus. Her daughter wrote that she met the Lord at Vacation Bible School when Mrs. Drayer gave an invitation to pray at the end of Bible story time. That is the specific time etched on her heart when she gave her life to Jesus, and she wanted me to know.

Her story tenderly touched my heart and encouraged me very much. I needed to hear those words, since I had been praying about and planning for our church's upcoming VBS. What we did and said during this special event truly did make a difference in the lives of children, and God worked through our efforts in ways we never knew. These positive words strengthened my faith as I was about to head out on my quiet retreat with the Lord.

Later that same evening, the Lord spoke to me through a lovely young lady who gave a speech at the awards ceremony. This student was a senior, ready to graduate and move onto her next phase in life. Her points were bold and confident, and four words resonated in my soul ... "*What is your story?*"

This sounded familiar, since God had called me to write years ago, but I hadn't known how to start. She proceeded to say, "*don't be afraid to take a chance in life,*" explaining how fear has the ability to paralyze, as it had in her early years of high school. She said to "*punch fear in the face!*" A pretty strong statement, but I liked it. It had truth. It had power. The enemy wants us to be afraid to take a step of faith. However,

"*God did not give us a spirit of fear, but of
power, and of love, and of a sound mind.*"
(2 Timothy 1:7)

We are much safer in the will of God, even in the simple comings and goings of life, than living outside of His will. By attending the awards ceremony with my son, I not only got to applaud his amazing achievement, but the Lord blessed and encouraged me as well.

We must diligently seek His voice and surrender our schedules so we can clearly see and hear. We can feel peace through this kind of relationship in the midst of a busy season in life. This prayer is worth repeating. *"God, what would you have me do?"*

When we want to control it all and never seek the Lord's counsel, it is then we spiral out of control, feeling helpless and agitated. We are unable to serve with a loving heart and positive attitude. When we give our schedule to Him, He rewards us with exactly what we need.

You might be thinking, *"Nicole, you don't understand my schedule. I cannot simply pick up and go away on retreat."* Do you think it was easy for me? *"Nicole, you do not know how busy my family is. It's different."* Is it, really? Consider these scriptures:

"This is love, that we walk according to His
commandment ..."
(2 John 1:6)

"Blessed are those who
hear the word of God and keep it."
(Luke 11:28)

What is He asking YOU specifically to do? What is *HE* asking *YOU* to give up? Obedience looks different for each one of us because He calls us to do different things. No, we are not all called to go away on a quiet retreat or to write a book; but we are called to something specific the Lord designed just for us.

Something I have learned on my journey is to be thankful for and seize the opportunities the Lord puts in my path and to appreciate the privilege to join God in His plans.

Draw Near to God

That peaceful time at the retreat center couldn't last forever. And my grand, studious writing desk with a breathtaking view turned into my kitchen table with my little boy's dusty baseball cap sitting right next to me. The smell of hamburger still lingers in the air from dinner. Dishes remain stacked in the sink; my faithful dog lies by my side, and the faint noise of the television carries down the hall. The everyday duties of life are reality once again as I have come down from the mountain. Literally. The noise of life has re-entered my world.

It is good that I obeyed the Father to *"be still"* in His presence—to listen and surrender to the call. I feel confident, refreshed, and strengthened. I have clarity and understanding. And because this was true rest in Him, it was also very productive through the writing of this book. I'm truly thankful because I realized I simply had to draw near to Him. And guess what? He drew near to me in return (James 4:8)!

I share this because even though I, like you, have a multitude of responsibilities in life ... I finally listened to the Lord, surrendered my schedule, took a step of faith, and put Him first. I followed Him in obedience to a quiet time, away from the noise and distractions of life to receive and believe what He had for me. As it says in Jeremiah 29:13,

> *"You will seek me and find me when you
> search for me with all your heart."*

We must be intentional in our desire to spend time with the Lord. It's very much related to a marriage relationship or close friendship. How can people remain connected when *both* parties neglect to speak, listen, and be in each other's *presence?* How can any relationship stay strong or grow without communication and intimacy?

We need this time with God or we'll begin to drift away into the deep waters of life. The noise will begin to drown out the voice of our Lord. We will begin to feel distant, almost like a stranger to Him, because we've let other people, events, and activities take the place of our time alone with the Father. Even Jesus himself, although active in His faith and teaching, took time away on a number of occasions.

> *"So He Himself often withdrew into the
> wilderness and prayed." (Luke 5:16)*

> *"Now in the morning, having risen a long
> while before daylight, He went out and
> departed to a solitary place; and there He
> prayed." (Mark 1:35)*

"Immediately He made His disciples get into
the boat and go before Him to the other side,
to Bethsaida, while He sent the multitude
away. And when He had sent them away, He
departed to the mountain to pray."
(Mark 6:45-46)

We must be deliberate and draw near to God. Then, when we confess the obstacles we've let get in the way of our relationship with Him, He will begin to break down the barriers and draw near to us. We must be aware of, confess, and repent of our overloaded schedules and give up our selfish tendencies with our time.

Live in and Enjoy the God-Given Moments

We must live in the God-given moments and be aware of what the Lord is doing in and around us. Experience His presence and beauty all around. We must slow down and open our eyes to see Him in a blooming tree, a dancing butterfly, a graceful deer, a friendly smile, a kind gesture, and a child's laughter. Or like me, it was in the so-called *"chance"* meeting of an old friend.

I used to live life in such a structured way, checking off each duty that needed accomplished — not wanting to get off task or leave something incomplete. In fact, I lived *so* regimented that I missed out on some of my children's younger years of development and special moments.

I remember my daughter, Eden, once told me that she had an odd dream. She was with me in a card store and a huge bear walked in. Others panicked, and she tried to get my attention. But I never looked once or answered her. I was oblivious to what was happening. It dawned on me that this dream was a reflection of my life through my daughter's eyes. I needed to learn to stop my plans, let some things go, and see what was really important. Yes, we honor God by keeping our homes and taking care of the blessings He's so graciously given us, but not at the cost of our families, loved ones, or the lost.

Jesus talks about this very thing when the Pharisees questioned Him for healing on the Sabbath. Mark 3:4-5 reads,

> *"Then He said to them, 'Is it lawful on the Sabbath to do good or to do evil, to save life or to kill?' But they kept silent. And when He had looked around at them with anger, being grieved by the hardness of their hearts, He said to the man, 'Stretch out your hand.' And he stretched it out, and his hand was restored as whole as the other."*

What was more important? Rules or people? I don't know about you, but I sure don't want to do evil in the eyes of the Lord or have a stubborn heart! I want to see with His eyes, love with His great love, and yield my schedule to His mighty will.

Friend, we should be honored to join our Lord in carrying out His purposes and plans. It is so others would be saved and our Father glorified! Take some time to bring your busy schedule and hectic life to Him. Are you feeling frazzled and out of control? Leave it there at the altar as a sacrifice, and ask Him to speak clearly to you about what to change, give up, or rearrange. What can you reorganize in order to give the Savior more of your time? The time He *deserves*.

Here are three steps to remember:

- **Submit** your schedule.

- **Seek** the Lord.

- **Pray** for direction about what to keep and what to eliminate.

Submit. Seek. Pray. Ask Him for His strength to obey and follow through. Please don't let your calendar dictate your life anymore! As you let go and let God be the master of your schedule, you will begin to feel peace.

Nicole Drayer

Chapter 7
The Pieces of My Time

When I first got on Facebook, it was a fun way to connect to old and new friends and relatives, reveal what was going on in our family lives, share about Christ, or offer positive words.

Over time, I was so drawn in and addicted that it stole time away from my husband, children, and friends. I had the need to check my status constantly, and I never lived in the moment. It created some ugly things in my heart—things I would never admit happened to me. I became judgmental and critical. *"Why are they wearing that?"* *"Why did they post 20 times today?"* I became jealous. *"Wow, they have so many likes."* *"Just look how pretty they are."* *"I wish I lived in a house like that."* *"Why aren't they responding to me? What did I do?"*

What is all of this? Pride, jealousy, greed, negativity, and narcissism. It is ugliness at its worst and not Christ-like at all. Not only was I wasting time, but there was evil in my heart.

Now please hear me, this is my own personal conviction and opinion. God spoke loud and clear to me on this specific issue. I was at a women's retreat, and the speaker, author Melissa Deming, spoke of kingdom hearts:

"A busy heart is a divided heart, and a divided heart cannot be a kingdom heart."

This really cut deep within me as I felt conviction. God spoke loud and clear about some changes I needed to make, starting with social media. I had to get off Facebook immediately. It could not be clearer to me. Up until this point, God had prompted and nudged me for months, but I disobeyed. When focused on His word during the retreat, His message penetrated deep within—I felt it in my gut.

My heart was pounding, and I knew it had to be done. At first, I couldn't figure out how to deactivate my account, but my husband helped me to do so when I arrived home the next day. I cut myself off from the social world for three months.

For me, getting off Facebook was more than whether it was right or wrong to have an account. It was about being obedient to God's voice in my life. It was about dying to self. Each one of us is different with diverse issues, addictions, bondages, and sin problems. I simply disobeyed the Lord by wasting my God-given time on social media and making idols out of it and my smartphone.

So, I went cold turkey and shut down my account. What did I find? Peace. And I had more time. God showed me that I could function without always checking in and finding approval from my Facebook audience. He proved once again that He was the only audience that truly mattered.

The next step was rearranging the use of my phone. It is my alarm clock, so it is the first thing I grab when I wake up. Each morning I pick up my device, and after checking the time, I either jump on Facebook or check my text messages or emails. Through the Holy Spirit's conviction, I was once again reminded that God was a jealous God (Exodus 34:14).

So instead of checking social media after I shut off my alarm and check the time, I now thank Him for the day. Then I continue with my daily routine. *Give Him the time He indeed deserves before you move onto the next thing.* Pray and read the Bible first. So simple, yet so critical.

Wait ... you don't think you have time? Making or wasting time is a decision. You can stay up too late, then hit snooze five times before you have to jump out of bed and rush to get out of the house on time, without an extra minute to spare. Or, decide to go to bed at a more reasonable time, and get up earlier to create more time to spend with Him.

God deserves our best, our all, our time, the first moments—every moment—of our day. Ask Him to help you be alert so you can see who and what He puts in your path for that specific day. To look outwardly, not only within. Ask Him questions like *"God, what should I do with my time today?"* or *"How can I use it for your glory?"* Ask Him ... you will be amazed at what He brings your way!

After months of detachment from Facebook and disciplining myself to seek Him first, God gave me the OK to get back on social media again. What did I learn? I am not addicted or consumed with it. I can use it in a healthy and fun manner to remain connected to friends and family, while sharing the gospel of Christ. If I feel my old sinful ways creeping in, I follow the Holy Spirit's lead and take a break.

We all have issues with something that too easily takes the place of God in our lives. And when it soaks up all of our time, it becomes a problem. Mine was my phone and social media. What is it for you? What is wasting your time and taking your focus off of Christ? What do you need to give up?

How Does God Want You to Spend Your Time?

When you stay connected to God, He directs your time. But, how can we know what He wants of us if we are not in the word daily, in close relationship to other believers, serving in a ministry, or attending church on a consistent basis? These are things that are extremely important to the life of a Christian; to think otherwise is concerning. In John 15:5, Jesus says,

> *"I am the vine, you are the branches. He who*
> *abides in Me, and I in him, bears much fruit;*
> *for without Me you can do nothing."*

"Without me, you can do nothing!" Are you connected to Jesus? I know this is difficult to face, but we must pray, self-reflect, and be aware of our relationship with the Lord and how we are attached, growing, and being used to share His love with others.

It's essential to read the Bible daily. *Daily.* It is ridiculous to think we can live like Christ if we don't know His teaching. How can we know God's thoughts, learn His lessons, gain His wisdom, and really know the heart of God otherwise?

There was a time that I didn't do this—even as a Christian. Did I turn away from God? No. Did I lose my salvation? No. Did I love Him less? No. However, I wasn't in a close relationship with Him. I felt distant, but it was because of me. I allowed my earthly and selfish thoughts to rule over me rather than God's thoughts. I was driven by other things in this life. Did I read my Bible or devotionals? Yes ... but inconsistently. Did I go to church and participate in ministry? Yes. BUT I was still far from God.

Please hear me, friend ... we need to be in the scriptures daily to live by God's wisdom, strength, discernment, and truth. Why do we feel that we can't hear from God? Are we reading His word and praying daily? Are we listening to God daily? Are we meeting with other believers to disciple and learn from? Oh boy, we sure can fit lots and lots of other things in to fill up our time ... other than God and His word. If you don't know His word, then you don't know that His word is a lamp to your feet and a light to your path. And you wouldn't know His initial instruction for Christian living:

> *"Then Jesus said to those ... who believed Him,*
> *'If you abide in My word, you are My disciples*
> *indeed. And you shall know the truth, and the*
> *truth shall make you free.'"*
> *(John 8:31-32)*

At our elementary school, the kids are allowed to buy *"extras"* after they eat their main lunch—a drink, chips, snacks, or a dessert. So, what if your child *only* ate *"extras"* at school every single day? Would that be healthy? Would they get satisfied or filled up with chips, fruit snacks, and ice cream bars? Is this the best nutritional choice for their growth? I think you would agree it isn't.

So now let's relate that example to daily Bible reading. I like to think of special devotionals, Christian books, and sermon videos as *"extras."* The Bible, God's Word, is the main course. Sure, these supplemental materials are good and can teach a lot, but they don't nourish our souls or give us strength for spiritual growth like the Bible. We need its Truth to turn away from sin and choose God's way—to know light from darkness and to stand firm in the faith.

Are you getting a steady diet of God's Word ... daily? When I learned this lesson in my own life, it was one of the pivotal moments in my faith. A time in which I began to change and grow in deep and meaningful ways! Ways in which passion for the Lord, His Word, and His ways returned to me. Closeness to the Savior was rekindled. My eyes were once again able to clearly see His works and my ears were opened to His voice.

It's also essential to get connected to a friend for discipleship. Pray and read the Bible together on a weekly basis, in addition to your own personal reading. You can both learn from each other as you hold one another accountable. When we are connected to the vine (God) through fellowship and discipleship, incredible things begin to happen. Further, find a good Bible teaching and believing church in which you can share your gifts and go make disciples.

It's not about getting saved and then hoarding our faith in Christ all to ourselves. It's not about giving our lives to Christ and then living as a slave to our children, running them all over creation to their activities. It is about so much more than us. It is first about our Lord and Savior and then about sharing the gospel with others. We are not meant to do all this alone and in isolation. Look at Jesus. He had His 12 disciples with Him as He ministered and shared the Truth.

He's Making Something New and Beautiful in His Time

Have you ever felt like God wanted you to do something, but it took forever to come to fruition? Or perhaps it hasn't happened, yet. Do you ever feel like you are not fulfilling the things in life you were meant to accomplish? You've been waiting on God to reveal His plan for your life, but it feels like time stands still. Oh, I know waiting isn't fun. But guess what? There is beauty in waiting. Why? He is making something new. Right now, in the waiting, the desert, the monotony, the lull … He is making something beautiful.

There is a song by a Christian band, Gungor, called *Beautiful Things*. I love this song. A few of the lyrics go like this,

"You make beautiful things, You make beautiful
things out of the dust. You make beautiful

things, You make beautiful things out of us."

What an awesome God we serve when even in our sin and human selfishness, He forgives and transforms us into something brand new ... *even better than before!* He desires to use us to fulfill His purposes and plans. Praise God for His grace, wisdom, plan, mighty love, and unexplainable power!

Think of some of the Bible accounts in which people waited to complete the task God called them to. After years of preparation and wonder, God used them in His perfect timing to do unbelievable and unexplainable things. How long did Noah wait for rain? Moses and the Israelites wandered for 40 years in the desert. Joseph sat in prison, not realizing one day he would be favored in the eyes of Pharaoh and would rescue his family in a miraculous way. Sarah waited a lifetime for a baby. Jesus himself did not begin ministry until he was in His 30s. Following Jesus' crucifixion, the disciples sat, prayed, and waited in the upper room. God was doing something within each of them while they waited, preparing them for the mission ahead. What mission lies ahead in your own life? What is our Savior preparing you for? **Spend some time praying about it and write down your thoughts...**

_____

_____

_____

_____

_____

_____

_____

_____

_____

_____

_____

_____

_____

_____

_____

_____

_____

_____

Spiritual Growing Pains

I love to walk. I grew up watching my mom walk at our local track and all throughout the neighborhood. I followed in her steps as my favored form of exercise. Even though I've spent many boring hours on my treadmill, my favorite place to walk is in the park behind our house. We are blessed with beautiful woods filled with hiking trails and various paths right in our backyard. When I walk outside in nature, I feel the presence of God all around me. This is where I love to talk to the Lord and listen to Him speak.

People have different places where they feel and meet with God, but the beauty of nature is my special meeting place with Jesus. This past summer, the Lord revealed much of what I am writing in this book, just by taking a walk in the woods to seek His face and direction.

One warm spring day, I set out on an *"adventure,"* talking to God and enjoying the beauty all around me. Trees were budding, flowers were blooming; new life emerged. A tiny butterfly met me on a trail and led my way. As I gazed at one of God's wondrous creations, something occurred to me.

Although elementary and trivial, God revealed Himself to me through a butterfly. He reminded me that a butterfly starts out as a caterpillar, beautifully made by Him. It has its own special purpose and plan.

After it lives as a caterpillar for a while, it develops into a cocoon or chrysalis stage. A *"waiting"* stage. In this covering, the caterpillar waits. It is protected and attached to something while it waits and waits. It does nothing in its own power as it physically changes. It sits and remains, transforming and changing while it rests in this shell.

At the perfect time, the caterpillar emerges out of the cocoon into a spectacular new creation! It can spread its wings and fly! It is ready for a new adventure! It is ready for a new purpose and plan.

Then it hit me ... isn't it the same with us? We, like the butterfly, are beautiful creations made for a purpose. God uses us in many different ways, and life is good. Then change comes. Waiting. Praying. Waiting. Then more waiting. Wondering. Changing. Growing pains. Discomfort. It's difficult to understand, but we must remain in Him during this time of transition.

Covered by His mighty protection, we must attach to the *"vine"* of Jesus and our church body. We sit and anticipate, covered in prayer and protection of other believers. As we wait on the Lord, He transforms us from the inside out. Often times it hurts, and we are left wondering why these things happen.

During this process, we are changed into a new creation. He makes us new and ready for the next adventure ... the next part of our Father's plan. When we are ready in His perfect time, we can burst out as a new and even more beautiful creation. At this time, we are ready to spread our wings and fly, my friend.

There is beauty and purpose in waiting. We can now do things we were not ready or prepared for in the past. But we must go through this transition first. It is truly a beautiful thing! We are stronger and equipped for new ministry. It is all very, very good. Very hard at times, but very good. Do not lose hope or lose sight of the Savior during this time of waiting and transition.

It is much like giving birth. Sometimes we go through seasons in life that seem endless. We are waiting as God is developing something within us, just like a baby in a mother's womb. God speaks, and an idea is brought to our attention. It takes much time to grow and mature. Over this time, we face pain, discomfort, sleepless nights, and spurts of joy. As the pregnancy comes to an end, the labor pains begin. The Lord prepares us to finally give birth to the idea, the call, the new adventure that took all this time to develop! Trust Him in the waiting. He has a purpose.

As I wrote this chapter, I was going through change—change I never thought would occur in the way it did. God always seems to surprise us, doesn't He? I recently told my friend that it *must* be of God when it seems to not make sense at all, or our circumstance is very difficult and unexpected. Why? God wants to wow us. He wants us to rely on Him in such a way that His glory is revealed and shines through our situation.

When I began my writing adventure, I had just finished up my sixth-year teaching preschool. This job was a beautiful blessing to me. I was doing what I loved to do, what God created me to do. I desired to be a teacher ever since I was a little girl. I, just like my daughter does now, would play school for hours.

This dream came to fruition as I taught special education for about five years before Greg and I started our family. Not only did I view this job as a ministry to children and families, but I, too, received many blessings from this special time in my life. It was so much fun!

Every day I loved going to my job, working with amazing women and children in a nurturing place. It was easy for me because it was natural. It was safe. I was happy and content. I had friends to talk to and pray with if needed. We laughed, and we cried. We lived life together and shared in ministry.

As the school year came to an end, I surrendered to God and obeyed the call to go on the private prayer retreat I wrote about in the last chapter. Although I thought He was leading me to write, I had no idea what the Lord truly had in store for me.

As my summer unraveled, so did my safe consistent life I once knew. I had previously prayed for a summer job. I did not get paid throughout the summer at the preschool, so I always searched for something to supplement that income.

The Lord led me to a place I thought would provide a flexible schedule, giving me time to serve while working. I took a job as a caregiver for senior citizens. After I trained, the manager and owner of the company called me in to ask if I would like to work in the office instead. This was a totally unexpected surprise to me. I was able to work 8 AM to noon every day and then come home to my children. My job would be answering phones, job recruiting, and interviewing possible candidates for caregiver positions.

During this time, the Lord was decreasing my appetite for the preschool. I felt a strong prompting from the Lord to remain at this new place of employment, but I didn't understand why.

As I yielded to the call to write my story, God led me down a completely different path. The Lord was showing me that, although I will always have a deep love and passion for children, He had something different in mind during this particular season.

As summer drew to an end, so did my short hours at the office. It was at that time my boss offered me a full-time position. New opportunities kept coming, and my life swiftly changed. After talking and praying with my husband, the Lord also revealed that He wanted me to step away from leading the children's ministry at church to allow others to pour their passion into children. This was all a lot to take in. It was very difficult to process. It didn't come naturally and felt very new and different.

I stepped out in faith and obedience onto the waves of the unknown, realizing I must keep my eyes on Jesus, or I would sink. I prayed and sought God every day as I grieved the loss of a job that I dearly loved, trying to see what the Lord had for me in this new area of my life.

I share all of this personal experience because once again, we can and will have the peace of Christ when we submit and give our time, schedule, hopes, and dreams over to Him. We need to stay connected so we grow. Then we must GO, obedient to His call and lead ... wherever that may be.

Time to Get Real

What you must do now is get honest about your time. The Lord knows your heart anyway. You cannot hide the truth from Him. He knows your struggles. Search your heart, and ask the Lord to reveal the chaos that must come to an end.

> *"For God is not the author of confusion but of peace ..." (1 Corinthians 14:33)*

So, where is the Holy Spirit leading you? Have you been waiting? Are you confused, scared, worried, burdened? Give it all over to Him. He knows your thoughts, anyway. Be honest. Cry out to the Lord, and He will answer you!

> *"The righteous cry out, and the Lord hears them; He delivers them out of all their troubles." (Psalm 34:17)*

Write a prayer of confession at the end of this chapter. Be honest about the things that take over your time in an unhealthy way: your busy schedule, inconsistencies, and what it is you are waiting for. Ask Him for wisdom on how to manage your time better. Let Him minister to you and heal you. Ask the Lord to help you see and understand your circumstances. As you pour out your heart, may you receive His beautiful peace.

_____
_____
_____
_____
_____
_____
_____
_____
_____
_____
_____
_____
_____
_____
_____
_____
_____
_____
_____
_____
_____
_____
_____
_____

Chapter 8
The Pieces of Pride

*I*t was a beautiful day, and Greg, our three children, and I drove down to the park behind our house. The kids were playing and learning to ride their bikes. But what started as a lovely evening soon turned into a mess. Our oldest son Caleb, who has a very strong will, was butting heads with Greg. My husband is very even keeled and is not easily angered. Our oldest son was pressing us on some issues, which turned into disaster. He doesn't easily accept help, and nothing we say ever seems to phase or change his mind.

On this particular day, Caleb was feeling defeated at not being able to ride his bike and wanted to give up. Greg was simply trying to push and encourage him. I could see my son's whole being crumble as he argued with my husband. As a mom ... the nurturer and comforter ... this moment was hard to watch. This is when I quickly jumped in with my two cents. *"He thinks you don't think he is smart!"* Without thinking and using discernment, I acted out on a whim. And even though I knew that is not what my husband meant, all my son heard was: *Daddy thinks I'm dumb.*

My husband and son were both broken. I disrespected my husband and his authority over the issue with our son. If I had thought about my actions first, I would've asked my husband to step aside and speak to him alone, rather than challenge his discipline and discredit our front as a parental team. It's taken me years to learn to do this. *(Did I say years? OK, I'm still learning!)*

My seemingly small, off-the-cuff statement escalated the situation to the point of aggravation, anger, frustration, and to my son breaking down in tears. We left as my husband abruptly packed up the van with the bicycles; you could hear a pin drop on the ride home. You could literally cut the tension with a knife. I knew, just knew, my husband was angry with me. I said some hurtful things without thinking, and I couldn't take them back.

Once we got home and the kids scattered to their corners of the house, my husband said he was really upset and that we needed to talk now. Before I go on, let me quickly rewind to earlier that day, when my dear friend Julie and I met for Bible study. We were studying Ephesians and read these verses:

> *"In your anger do not sin: Do not let the sun go down while you are still angry ..."* (4:26)

I shared with Julie how Greg and I try our best to live by that, and it is important to us. Wow! God was preparing my heart to stand firm through that argument and yield to God's way over my own selfish pride. However, when Greg said he wanted to talk, I knew at that time I wasn't ready. He was quite agitated, and I was feeling anxious and ready to fly off the handle. So, I told him I couldn't talk at that moment and needed some alone time to pray first. I slipped upstairs to our room, shut the door, and got down on my knees. My heart was beating out of my chest, and I kept repeating, *"In your anger do not sin. In your anger do not sin…"* I submitted to the Lord and poured it all out to Him, confessing my prideful heart and asking for His peace and direction. I begged for Him to help us resolve our argument.

Greg and I finally came together, and God gave me the strength to say two simple words: *"I'm sorry."* He cried, and I cried. We held each other and talked. We prayed. You see, I was never the one to admit I was wrong first. The prideful part of me always needed to be right and to be heard.

"Pride is sin, and it keeps us from complete and total surrender to the Lord."

God told me to put my husband first and to not sin in my anger. He gave me the strength and wisdom from His word to fight off the enemy. Greg then talked and prayed with Caleb, and there was peace once again. And that evening, God overcame pride with peace that ruled in our hearts and home.

Understanding Pride

Pride, at its core, is *"a feeling or deep pleasure or satisfaction derived from one's own achievements."* I have been molded most of my Christian life to believe that I should *not* be proud of myself; but I can, in fact, be proud of my children, my husband, friends, or family. I am left wondering, what does God say about all of this? According to 2 Timothy 3:1-4,

> *"...But know this, that in the last days perilous*
> *times will come: For men will be lovers of*
> *themselves, lovers of money, boasters, proud,*
> *blasphemers, disobedient to parents,*
> *unthankful, unholy, unloving, unforgiving,*
> *slanderers, without self-control, brutal,*
> *despisers of good, traitors, headstrong,*
> *haughty, lovers of pleasure rather than lovers*
> *of God ..."*

We do not like to think of ourselves as selfish beings or any of the aforementioned adjectives for that matter. But in reality, we are. I know you might think that's a pretty harsh statement. However, this has been the case from the very beginning when Eve ate the fruit and blamed Adam for her actions. Cain killed his brother Abel because of pride and jealousy. I pridefully put down my husband. And I bet you can fill in the blanks, too.

Friend, we live in such a *"seeking-self-pleasure-and-it's-all-about me"* age, and sometimes we don't even realize it. We want to look prettier and be thinner and know *ALL* the answers; we want to own the right clothes because we must feel good about ourselves no matter the cost.

It causes us to be immersed in social media, living a fantasy on Facebook and obsessing with selfies. Yes, we are to care for and love the person Jesus died for, but there is a difference between loving and caring for ourselves and being infatuated with self. Our agendas can be driven by all our inward preoccupations if we're not careful.

Pride is sin, and it keeps us from complete and total surrender to the Lord. We need to recognize this for what it is in our personal lives, families, homes, and churches and begin to tear down the walls of conceit. It's these barriers that keep us separated from others by living life in a self-focused manner that is opposite of what Jesus asks us to do.

To live outwardly focused means we want to help the world for the *right* reasons. Not for our own gain or to make ourselves look good, but for the Glory of God so that others might be saved.

We Are All Guilty of Being Selfish

I've been brought to my knees more than once to confess aspects of narcissism *(fascination with oneself)* in my own life. The Lord convicted me about this self-centeredness through how I dealt with my husband, coworkers, family, as well as when I wrestled with my appearance. Do these behaviors sound familiar: a controlling attitude, thriving on the praise of people, worrying about appearance, carrying a fragile ego?

Oh, how I've struggled with these issues at one time or another. I discovered one of those negative attributes a few years back. At the pre-school, I thrived on the praise of parents and families who thought I did an amazing job teaching their children. It gave me a sense of self-worth and dignity to know I was thought of in such a high and well-respected manner—to the point where it went to my head a little too much! But then we can mask these types of thoughts as *"false humility,"* as I would never admit my narcissistic tendencies to anyone. It's all too easy to tuck selfish feelings way down deep for no one to know about.

We have to search our hearts for the reasons behind our deep need to be heard, seen, or noticed. For most of my life I felt insecure, inadequate, or not good enough. It's important to make sure that the pendulum in life does not swing from one end of the spectrum to the other.

A Healthy Balance

In her book, *He Speaks to Me,* author and speaker Priscilla Shirer provides a sound definition of humility: *"Knowing, accepting, and being yourself—your best self—for God's glory."*

She also suggests avoiding the extremes of pride and humility, including: *"thinking less of yourself than you ought to or thinking more of yourself than you ought to."*

The opposite of pride is humility, which is *"freedom of pride or arrogance: the quality or state of being humble."* Humble means *"showing a low-estimate of one's importance."*

The Bible speaks clearly about pride and humility. Proverbs 11:2 states,

"When pride comes, then comes shame: but with the humble is wisdom ..."

"A man's pride will bring him low, but the humble in spirit will retain honor."
(Proverbs 29:23).

We need to let Jesus be the one who consumes our hearts and be the driving factor on why we do things. He is the only audience that should matter. Jealousy and pride can make us do crazy things, so we need to keep our hearts in check.

Again, it comes down to this: we should never think too little or too high of ourselves. We need a healthy balance. I've learned over the years that my ways are not the only ways, and my time is not my own. Life is short, and we have to decide between wasting our days on selfish desires and ambitions or living in such a way that the Lord will direct our every move. Do you want to waste it on foolish things or invest it in eternal things?

The realization of pride in my everyday life has been a wake-up call for me. I discovered pride is what brings about most disagreements and builds unnecessary walls—not only in marriage, but in friendships, working relationships, and with other family members. I am learning how to truly respect my husband and hold my tongue when things are difficult, taking the wise advice from Proverbs 15:1,

"A soft answer turns away wrath..."

A social media post by pastor and author Louie Giglio also caught my attention: *"Maturing is realizing how many things do not require your comment."*

Ouch. I felt that one, how about you? I have always needed to have the last word. Why? Pride. I can feel good for the few minutes after I've *"won"* the battle, but that feeling doesn't last. It quickly turns into sadness, shame, and isolation because it was borne out of sin.

Even in Christian circles of friends, I can feel insecurity rising. Most times women want to fix problems and have all the answers. We want to be able to give the best advice or encouragement and be the heroine for the day! We want to seem well educated in scripture so others look to us. But who *should* get all of the credit and be the hero? Jesus! I'm learning that we have two ears to hear and one mouth to speak. It's time to lay pride aside, listening twice as much as we talk.

Pride, my friend, is really a heart issue. We need to look at, confess, repent, and surrender it once and for all. This is a significant piece that we may be able to mask for others, but certainly not for God. He sees the human heart as it is.

Take a Closer Look at Your Heart

When I looked up the definition of *heart*, not only did I find the physical tissue explanation but a more profound meaning. *Heart* can also mean the *"central or innermost part"* or the *"vital part or essence of."*

When you look up the word *essence,* you will find synonyms such as soul, spirit, or core. Now we're getting somewhere! This small, extremely durable and necessary organ is also the central core of who we are. To put it all together, I see our physical heart as very strong and significant to life in general, but our nonphysical heart is so much more.

I view it as an extremely fragile, sensitive, vulnerable, and vital entity to our spiritual existence and relationship with the Father. So, when you read the words in Luke 10:27 that tell you to ...

"Love the LORD your God with all your heart,
with all your soul, with all your strength, and
with all your mind, and your neighbor as
yourself ..."

... you can perceive the much deeper meaning. Love God with your spirit—the entire central core of who you are—from deep within. This small organ is essential and strong, yet delicate and vulnerable.

As you daily surrender the pieces of your heart to God, here are some thoughts and scripture to meditate on. Search your heart deeply, and if pride is something you struggle with, give this piece of your life over to God and allow His peace and freedom to wash over you.

1. **God's Heart**: He first loved us! Thank you, Lord!

   *"For God so loved the world that He gave His
   only begotten Son, that whoever believes in
   Him should not perish but have everlasting
   life." (John 3:16)*

2. **Your Heart:** When we <u>surrender</u> our lives to Christ, He transforms us and gives us a <u>new heart</u>!

   *"I will give you a new heart and put a new
   spirit within you; I will take the heart of stone
   ... and give you a heart of flesh."
   (Ezekiel 36:26)*

   *"You will find Me, when you search for Me
   with all your heart." (Jeremiah 29:13)*

3. **God First:** We are to put Him first in our lives above all else.

   *"Love the LORD your God with all your heart,
   with all your soul, with all your strength, and
   with all your mind, and your neighbor as
   yourself ..." Luke 10:27*

4. **Communication:** We need to talk to God daily through <u>prayer.</u> <u>Confess, repent, and be real</u>. He knows your heart, anyway!

*"Search me, O God, and know my heart; Try
me, and know my anxieties."*
(Psalm 139:23)

"The heart is deceitful above all things,
*And desperately wicked; Who can know it?
I, the* LORD, *search the heart, I test the mind,
Even to give every man according to his ways,
According to the fruit of his doings."*
(Jeremiah 17:9-10)

*"Rejoice always, pray without ceasing, in
everything give thanks; for this is the will of
God in Christ Jesus for you."*
(1 Thessalonians 5:16-18)

*"Repent therefore and be converted, that your
sins may be blotted out, so that times of
refreshing may come from the presence of the
Lord ..." (Acts 3:19)*

5. **Guard Your Heart:** We must <u>protect and guard our hearts</u> because the enemy is out to destroy us. Be awake, alert, and aware!

*"Above all else, guard your heart, for
everything you do flows from it."*
(Proverbs 4:23)

"The weapons we fight with are not the weapons of the world. On the contrary, they have divine power to demolish strongholds."
(2 Corinthians 10:4)

6. **Love Others:** Because we love God, we are commanded to love others and serve Him.

"Dear children, let us not love with words or speech but with actions and in truth."
(1 John 3:18)

"Beloved, let us love one another, for love is of God; and everyone who loves is born of God and knows God. He who does not love does not know God, for God is love."
(1 John 4:7-8)

Chapter 9
The Pieces of God's Call

hen you think of *calling*, what thoughts come to mind? You may call a friend after work to catch up. You call your child to come do his homework or for her to come to the dinner table. *Calling*, for any reason, elicits some kind of response. Your friend, to answer the phone or call back. Your kids to obey.

It is much the same with God when *He* calls *us* to do something. He asks us to take action for His glory alone *(even though He could do whatever it is in a heartbeat, without our help.)* He expects us to respond in obedience, joining in His mighty plan. What an honor and a privilege.

Let's look at someone in the Bible who became incredibly familiar with God's call. We're introduced to Moses in the book of Exodus when he was a baby, born to an enslaved Hebrew family in Egypt. Let's just say, a baby Hebrew boy is not who you wanted to be during this time in history. In order to control the Hebrew population, Pharaoh ordered a decree, demanding all newborn Hebrew boys be thrown into the Nile River and killed. But Moses' mother couldn't possibly do this horrific act and instead hid him for three months. When she couldn't conceal his existence any longer, she lovingly placed baby Moses in a basket and sent it down the Nile, watching and hoping for his rescue.

In what you could say was divine intervention, Pharaoh's daughter discovered Moses and raised him as her own. He had a good life and safe upbringing. However, when Moses grew into an adult, he fled Egypt after killing an Egyptian guard in defense of a Hebrew slave. He departed to Midian where he met his wife and became a shepherd. This is where he had an encounter with God. It was an ordinary day, and he was out tending his father-in-law's flock. He was minding his own business, doing his daily duties, when his life was interrupted by a burning bush. When Moses spied this strange event, he went to get a closer look. It is then God calls his name. Twice. God explains to Moses that He's heard the cries of the Hebrews and was deeply concerned with their suffering. The kicker? God wants to use Moses to rescue His children from Egypt's tyranny. We pick up their exchange in Exodus 3:10-11.

"Come now ... and I will send you to Pharaoh that you may bring My people, the children of Israel, out of Egypt. "But Moses said to God, 'Who am I that I should go to Pharaoh, and that I should bring the children of Israel out of Egypt?'"

Moses doubted this call. He was uncertain about his capabilities, rationalizing all the *"what-ifs."* The Israelites will never believe me. I'm not eloquent enough. Moses even asked God to please send someone else!

We are a lot like Moses. God asks us to do remarkable things designed specifically for each one of us. But what is our usual response? We also hesitate and feel unqualified for the job. We tell God why we cannot do it. I don't feel so badly now, how about you? This great Bible figure—who accomplished astonishing things for God—didn't believe in himself at first, either.

Does this justify us to doubt all the time, so much so that it consumes us and turns into worry? No. However, it is comforting to see that we, as Christians, have similar stories. He saves us; He changes us; and He calls us.

To what does He call us? He desires each of us to do something unique. You may not feel equipped for what God calls you to do. But you are called, and God will always be with you. Your call may change throughout your life as you walk in obedience with God and accomplish given tasks along the way. Then He could very well call you to something else.

We have an active faith, my friend. Please do not misunderstand me. I'm not saying we have a *"works-based"* faith alone. We cannot earn our salvation; it is given freely as a gift. But faith without works is dead. I bring this up because when we are *called* to do something, we must act in response.

What Are You Called to Do?

Your calling is indeed another piece of yourself to give back to God. Sometimes you feel called to do something, and then it never happens. Perhaps you get angry with God and waste many days waiting and wondering, *"When and why, God?"*

Conversely, you may not know or understand what your call is. You say you want to do something for God, but don't know what to do. So instead of asking, moving forward, and living life ... you sit by and do nothing. You see, we all are born with specific gifts and talents to be used for the glory of God. Some of them are easy to see and understand. Others are unclear and out of the ordinary.

I have discovered that there are two main callings on my life at this time. God has called Greg and me to be generational curse breakers in our families. This is a huge responsibility, but one that has been and still is very clear to us. We come from a line of unsaved people, with a heritage of alcoholics and law breakers, drug dealers and drug users. God saved Greg and me to begin a heritage of God-fearing believers. Our three children, Caleb Matthew, Eden Grace, and Elijah Luke, are our promises from God. Our main goal right now is our family. These are two of our life verses for our children:

*"Praise the Lord! Blessed is the man who fears
the Lord, who delights greatly in His
commandments. His descendants will be
mighty on earth; the generation of the upright
will be blessed." (Psalm 112:1-2)*

"Therefore, you shall lay up these words of mine in your heart and in your soul, and bind them as a sign on your hand, and they shall be as frontlets between your eyes. You shall teach them to your children, speaking of them when you sit in your house, when you walk by the way, when you lie down, and when you rise up." (Deuteronomy 11:18-19)

God's call on my own life is to write. As I have mentioned, He placed this book on my heart 15 years ago when Caleb was born. I was a new mom and still young in the faith. Even though I knew God placed this prompting in my heart, it burned within me for years before it came to fruition. I knew it was there, but didn't know when and how this calling would come together. It didn't make sense to me, but I continued to live life using my gifts as I saw fit, wherever the Lord led me. I was first a wife, then a mother, a youth leader, a reading teacher, a children's ministry director, a preschool teacher, a tutor, a pastor's wife, a VBS director, a prayer partner, a friend, a daughter, a sister, an aunt, a neighbor, a job recruiter, a doer of everyday household chores, a substitute teacher, and now a writer.

God told me *15 years ago* that I had a story to tell; He wanted me to support and encourage women through it. I prayed all these years to be faithful in the small things, and then God would give me greater things. It was an absolutely crazy idea to me, as I am not formally trained to write. However, God's plans usually are out of the ordinary and unexplainable! Are we going to put our faith into action and obey or choose to run from the Lord's calling for us?

Get Real with God

Through living life and serving the Lord, I have grown in so many ways. He has pruned the dead and unhealthy *"branches"* of my life, making me more fruitful in sharing the Good News. I encourage you to not get impatient and frustrated. God has plans for your good and not to harm you. He knows what is best. And even when it's the most difficult situation you can ever imagine, He is there with you. You may be in the fire, but you will not get burned.

Over the years, He has been faithful as my rock, my redeemer, my righteousness, my friend, my peace, my comforter, my strength, my shield, and my hiding place. I praise Him for every trial and every achievement. I would not be who I am today if I had not gone through such deep waters. Though at times I felt like I was sinking, He never let me drown. He was there all along and will be to the end.

I urge *you* to take some time and get real with God. Take a day retreat, an hour walk by yourself, or get up an hour earlier than everyone else in your household ... *away from the noise of life.* Pray eagerly, dig into His Word, and ask for His wisdom. I pray you diligently seek the Lord for guidance and discover what He specifically wants you to accomplish in and through Him.

You have been given gifts and talents that shouldn't be wasted. You have a particular purpose and plan. God may not audibly speak to you as He did Moses, but He *will* speak to you. It could be through His word, Christian friends, a sermon, a song of praise, or a quiet time. Ask and listen. Then obey ... even when it seems misunderstood or difficult. Simply trust God and obey.

When I left my preschool job to work in human resources, it was a very difficult eight months for me. When I felt troubled, I focused on the verse God gave me to confirm leaving the preschool. It was Deuteronomy 1:6-7,

> *"You have dwelt long enough at this mountain. Turn and take your journey ..."*

I understood that I absolutely loved my job at the preschool, and it was certainly a mountaintop experience for me. However, I transitioned to a place that was very hard for me. I didn't completely understand why I was there until much later. But, when I pondered the words of the scripture... *"turn and take your journey,"* I realized that a journey isn't sedentary or stagnant. It's full of movement. It is a time of passing through.

As Christians, we are all on a journey from this life to the next. Some of us stay at the same home or workplace for many years. My story is different; that's why I know God has a sense of humor. I dislike change very much. It makes me uncomfortable, and I usually fight it every step of the way. However, God knows what is best for us. He puts us in situations that cause us to rely on Him, not our ability. He wants to shine through us in powerful ways, for all to see.

But doubt does creep in. Writing this book is one example. I look at my mess-of-a-life in the past and my present inadequacies, and I can't even fathom what God wants to do through me. I have doubted many times that I have anything of importance to say. But He has called me. My constant prayer of surrender has been,

> More of You, God, and less of me. Please give me Your wisdom and Your thoughts. And help me in my unbelief.

I finally submitted to the call to write when I studied the parable of the talents in Matthew 25:14-30. Though the original story Jesus told was about money, I believe the text has a very important application about God's call on our lives.

> "For the kingdom of heaven is like a man traveling to a far country, **who called his own servants and delivered his goods to them.** And to one he gave five talents, to another two, and to another one, **to each according to his own ability,** and immediately he went on a journey. Then he who had received the five talents went and traded with them, and made another five talents. And likewise, he who had received two gained two more also. **But he who had received one went and dug in the ground, and hid his lord's money.** After a

long time, the lord of those servants came and
settled accounts with them.

"So, he who had received five talents came and
brought five other talents, saying, 'Lord, you
delivered to me five talents; look, I have gained five
more talents besides them.' His lord said to him,
'Well done, good and faithful servant; you were
faithful over a few things, I will make you ruler
over many things. Enter into the joy of your lord.'

He also who had received two talents came and
said, 'Lord, you delivered to me two talents; look, I
have gained two more talents besides them.' His
lord said to him, 'Well done, good and faithful
servant; you have been faithful over a few things, I
will make you ruler over many things. Enter into
the joy of your lord.'

"Then he who had received the one talent came
and said, 'Lord, I knew you to be a hard man,
reaping where you have not sown, and gathering
where you have not scattered seed. **And I was
afraid, and went and hid your talent in the
ground.** Look, there you have what is yours.'

"But his lord answered and said to him, **'You
wicked and lazy servant,** you knew that I reap
where I have not sown, and gather where I have
not scattered seed. So, you ought to have deposited
my money with the bankers, and at my coming I
would have received back my own with interest.

So, take the talent from him, and give it to him who has ten talents.

'For to everyone who has, more will be given, and he will have abundance; but from him who does not have, even what he has will be taken away. And cast the unprofitable servant into the outer darkness. There will be weeping and gnashing of teeth.'"

I like to think of these talents as true God-given talents. Notice the words I bolded in this scripture. The master called the servants and entrusted them with something. The one servant was full of much fear, so he buried his talent in the ground. The master was not pleased with this behavior at all!

This Bible story convicted me a while back. I simply did not believe I was to become a writer. I was too worried about the enormity of the task and was trying to hide and ignore it. Fortunately, I finally realized this was very wrong of me. I began to understand that God gave me a story to tell in order to give hope, and hiding was not the answer. I needed to submit and obey to His voice. I realized that I could not complete this task on my own, but only by His grace and power. This is when I began to dig up that which I had hidden. What talent do you have concealed? What God-given ability does the Lord want you to put into use and share?

The Challenge

We must lay down our calling—an extremely important and vital part of ourselves—and give it to Jesus. He knows best. His timing is perfect. He has a plan bigger and better than anything we could ever imagine or fathom. Remember,

"I can do all things through Christ who
strengthens me." (Philippians 4:13)

Your challenge is to seek the Lord diligently, asking Him what your call is. God may ask you to do the seemingly impossible, but remember all things are possible with God. In the nine months before I wrote this book, I went on two personal prayer retreats and left one job for another. All to follow God's call. Do I look crazy and unsettled to the world? Maybe. But I am following the Father. The disciples left everything behind to follow Jesus. I am reminded what Ruth says to her mother-in-law, Naomi …

"For wherever you go, I will go;
And wherever you lodge, I will lodge;
Your people shall be *my people,*
And your God, my God." (Ruth 1:16).

She followed where the Lord led her. Suffering death and famine, this decision may have seemed foolish, but it was Ruth's call to stay and care for Naomi. Won't you follow Him and answer the call on your life? For you, it might be a major life decision. Perhaps God is calling you to move, quit a job, start a business, go into missions, end a relationship, start a ministry, give money to help someone, sell your house, or foster a child. Or maybe it's time to take a smaller step towards the bigger picture.

Remember, when God calls you, He is with you and will equip you with everything you need to fulfill His purpose and plan. Is it easy? No. It requires a lot of sacrifice. Won't you seek, ask, surrender, and obey? You will be full of peace and joy to know you are walking in obedience to God.

"For to this you have been called, because
Christ also suffered for us, leaving us as an
example, that you should follow his steps."
(1 Peter 2:21)

"You did not choose me but I chose you, and
appointed you that you would go and bear
fruit, and that your fruit should remain,
that whatever you ask the Father
in my name He may give you."
(John 15:16)

Chapter 10
Peace by Piece: A Journey

In 2008, we were a family of four. Greg and I felt very happy and blessed. We were in our early 30s, faced with the question of whether or not we were finished having children. We were beyond grateful for the healthy little boy and girl we were entrusted to raise. However, we were not exactly certain what plans God had for us, so we didn't necessarily make it our goal to try for another child. But we didn't make a great effort to prevent our family from growing either.

We both agreed to put the possibility of having a third child in the Lord's hands and waited to see where He led. It did not take very long to receive the answer to our prayer. Our third child was born in August 2009.

I share this story because, even though we were not completely sure of what the Lord had in store for our family, Greg and I felt an uncertainty with the idea of not having any more children. Something did not feel quite right. Our family was not complete until we had Elijah Luke. We experienced a lack of peace because God's plan wasn't fulfilled for us. Once

Eli came along, we felt a warm sense of relief ... like we could let out a big sigh and continue with life as we knew it. We had peace.

Peace is a gift from the Lord. It is also one of the fruits of the spirit we produce when connected to Christ. In Hebrew, peace means *shalom* which is derived from the root representing *wholeness* or *completeness*. I love that! When we have the peace of Christ, we feel tranquil and complete. We are made whole, like Greg and I felt when we submitted our family to the Lord, and He entrusted us with Elijah.

Only Jesus Has the Power to Heal and Make Us New

Are you willing to let go and begin to live Peace by Piece? When we surrender all the broken pieces of our lives that we'd rather not give up—the fragments that control us and even the *"everyday"* shards—then we can be made whole. Peace is a gift from God. Yet, so many times in life, we hold tight to baggage from our past or present-day problems because we think we can handle them on our own. We find ourselves overburdened, unable to take on anything more, because our hands are so full of unnecessary gear. We are unable to accept any more gifts— even ones that are necessary and beneficial to us—because there is so much clutter.

If our hands are desperately grasping at *"parcels"* we have no business carrying around, how can we receive the gift of peace that Jesus so freely gives with open arms?

It's vital to let go of these hindrances and lay them down. Then you'll have room to ...

"Let the peace of Christ rule in your hearts."
(Colossians 3:15)

Remember, we need to be willing to make available space and *"let it?"*

We no longer have to live as slaves to our pasts or old lifestyles. I had walked in much darkness in the past, but the Lord became my light, my hope, and salvation.

Through complete surrender and the ability to let go, Jesus can break the chains that bind you, too. Although we ask Christ to be Lord of our lives, over time our sinful and self-focused tendencies take over; we tell Jesus what pieces of our lives He can have and keep other parts for ourselves. We sin and cause distance and barriers in our relationship with the Savior. We do indeed become bossy and micromanage our own lives. We completely take ownership of these areas and think we know better than God. This is where anxiety, stress, and imbalance come in. And when we subsequently don't feel peace, it's likely because we get in the way of God's plan for us.

Wrestling Can Bring Change
and Restore Peace

What I've learned, through experience, is that we need to include the Lord in every decision and motive, seeking the Holy

Spirit's counsel for direction and wisdom. It sometimes takes many lessons over for us to finally give a particular sin or circumstance back to Jesus and walk forward, free of all control.

But do you feel, more times than not, that you're in a wrestling match with the Lord over your own issues? I can relate. Although I know each concern belongs to Him, I still struggle with God over ownership of them. Fear, as I mentioned before, is a big stronghold for me. How about you? If you know it, name it. Or if you do not know your exact struggle, ask God to bring this issue to the surface. Come to a *point of realization* of this problem, take it to God, and then pray about resolving it.

What it comes to is *repentance* ... acknowledgement of a sin and then turning away from it once and for all. That is a huge step in the right direction! We should never remain stagnant in our relationship with God, even when it means wrestling with Him to gain a deeper understanding of His ways.

In Genesis 32:24-29, we learn about Esau and Jacob, the sons of Isaac and Rebekah. It was custom for the oldest son to receive the father's blessing, so naturally this should have been Esau. However, Jacob was favored by his mother, Rebekah, and Esau was favored by his father, Isaac. When Isaac was nearing the end of his life on earth, he asked Esau to kill some game and make him some stew. Then he would give him his blessing. Rebekah and Jacob devised a sneaky plan to fool Isaac. Jacob would disguise himself as Esau and bring him his meal. Since Isaac's sight was failing, he thought Jacob was the elder brother and gave him his blessing instead. When Esau found out, he became very angry to the point of wanting to kill his younger brother. But Jacob escaped Esau's tirade.

It took 20 years before Jacob returned home to restore *peace* with Esau. It was on his return expedition that Jacob wrestled with God over his baggage. Think about that for a second. He had the encounter with God *on his way back* to make things right. He chose to walk in the direction of restoration and forgiveness towards the Father. That's when he had a life altering encounter with the one true God.

You see, Jacob had his forefather's faith in the past, but was it his own faith? After Jacob wrestled with the Almighty, he was given the new name of Israel and was blessed. Let's look at this again ... while alone, years after a wrongdoing, Jacob struggled all through the night with the Holy One, was given a new name, and then blessed. After this personal experience with the Lord, peace was restored with his brother Esau, and then Jacob built an altar of thanksgiving and named it Israel.

God physically touched Jacob's hip during their *"wrestling match."* He spiritually touched me in a personal way through my heartache. And He can and will touch you and make *you* new as well.

What are you wrestling God about today? Give it over to Him because He is waiting to do something extraordinary in your life and restore peace once *again*. And although it might seem counterintuitive ... don't forget to *thank Him* for the struggle.

Sanctification and Growing Pains

Although our journey with the Lord is difficult, change, peace, and a beautiful closeness with Him occurs when we remain steadfast and strong in our faith—even through the trials. This brings us to a significant place for each believer, called *sanctification*.

> "Sanctification is the act or process of acquiring sanctity, of being made or becoming holy. It is a gift given through the power of God to a person or thing which is then considered sacred or set apart."

I love this! Sanctification is being set apart and made holy. This process takes an entire lifetime for us. We should allow God to transform and renew us continually if indeed we are children of God.

When I first gave my life to the Lord at 19, this process began. He gave me a new heart and the gift of the Holy Spirit. Although my transformation began very quickly, there was much I had to let go of, learn, and experience. It has taken years for me to get to this point, and God still has much work to do in me.

I like to think of sanctification as a refining process. Think about dirty water going through a purification system. This type of structure extracts and filters out all of the dangerous and harmful chemicals and impurities. Likewise, throughout our journey as a Christian, God constantly sanctifies and purifies us. He filters out all the debris and garbage that keep us from Him. He constantly makes us new, into His likeness.

I mentioned earlier that this process is also similar to having *growing pains*. God stretches and develops us in such a way that may hurt and feel uncomfortable for a little while. But then we are ready and prepared for the new phase of our journey ... stronger and better than before.

> *"Blessed is the one who perseveres under trial*
> *because, having stood the test, that person*
> *will receive the crown of life that the Lord has*
> *promised to those who love him."*
> *(James 1:12)*

> *"Consider it pure joy, my brothers and sisters,*
> *whenever you face trials of many kinds,*
> *because you know that the testing of your*
> *faith produces perseverance. Let perseverance*
> *finish its work so that you may be mature and*
> *complete, not lacking anything."*
> *(James 1:2-4)*

If you are a child of the King, you are being sanctified as well. As you experience these growing pains, are you resisting or allowing God to do His work within you?

Peace by Piece: A Journey

When I had the prompt to write so many years ago and more recently as I sat down to actually compose this book, I searched through my notes. I found some common verbiage.... *"God is my peace," "life is a journey,"* and *"Jesus has the supernatural ability to turn trials into triumphs."*

Much of what I shared in this book is hardships and difficulties God helped me have victory over and learn from ... in His strength and by His mighty power. Praise God!

An interesting thought that surfaced while reflecting on my life is my name means *"victorious."* Looking at my specific past and present troubles, I think this is a fitting reminder from God. And you can also know victory and peace, but not in your human ability. It is only by the supernatural power of our Mighty God, through the forgiveness and bloodshed of His Son, Jesus, and with the guidance of His Holy Spirit.

A lifelong journey is what we are on, friend. It's a journey with God—a journey of sanctification, of giving over our brokenness and shame, of healing, and of peace. We will never have complete peace until we are at home with the Father. However, we can indeed experience joy and peace, even in the midst of catastrophes, on this side of heaven because we know He is with us. He's got it. He can handle it. We need to trust Him and not in our own abilities. Give it all to Him, and press on.

My brokenness is not something I am proud of; however, it is a reality of the cross of Christ. We are all hurt and sick people in need of a Savior. We are perfectly imperfect people with shattered lives. My prayer is that you would grow into a deeper relationship with God than you've ever had before. I pray that you would earnestly seek Him and His ways for your life.

As you discover what areas you are clenching tightly to, let Him help you let go and give Him complete control. I hope and pray that you find healing from your past hurts and realize that you are loved and forgiven.

Once we stop fighting Him, we will have freedom and His beautiful peace. It is a gift He freely gives. Remember, you are not to walk this road alone. Surround yourself with a good solid group of Christian friends who love and support you. You no longer have to live in turmoil, stress, isolation, or darkness. Continue to soak up His word and pray without ceasing. Choose to live beautifully broken and accept the gift—Peace by Piece.

"For I know the plans I have for you," declares the Lord, "plans to prosper you and not to harm you, plans to give you hope and a future. Then you will call on me and come and pray to me, and I will listen to you. You will seek me and find me when you seek me with all your heart." Jeremiah 29:11-14

Attributions

CHAPTER 2: "I can see the ivy growing through the wall, 'cause you will stop at nothing to heal my broken soul. Faith is rising up like ivy, reaching for the light. Hope is stirring deep inside me, making all things right. Love is lifting me from sorrow catching every tear, dispelling every lie and torment crushing all my fears." Attribution: Jobe, K. (2017). "The Garden". The Garden [CD]. Sparrow Records. Brentwood, Tennessee.

CHAPTER 3: "In Hebrew, <u>delight</u> has several meanings: chaphets or 'to bend towards' and anag 'to be soft and delicate.' The root of <u>anag</u> is interesting because it means 'pliable.'" **Attribution:** Blue Bible Dictionary. www.blueletterbible.org

CHAPTER 3: "As the deer panteth for the water so my soul longeth after thee, you alone are my heart's desire and I long to worship thee. You alone are my strength my shield, to you alone may my spirit yield." **Attribution:** Martin J. Nystrom As the Deer lyrics © Universal Music Publishing Group, Capitol Christian Music Group

CHAPTER 5: "My friend wrote a book to encourage grieving siblings." **Attribution:** Wade, Z.R. (2013). My Story about You and Me, Author House. Bloomington, IN.

CHAPTER 7: "I was at a women's retreat, and the speaker, author Melissa Deming, spoke of Kingdom hearts: 'A busy heart is a divided heart, and a divided heart cannot be a kingdom heart.'" **Attribution:** Deming, Melissa.

CHAPTER 7: "You make beautiful things, You make beautiful things out of the dust. You make beautiful things, You make beautiful things out of us." **Attribution:** Gungor. (2010). "Beautiful Things". Beautiful Things [CD]. Lyrics © Capitol Christian Music Group.

CHAPTER 8: Social media post: "Maturing is realizing how many things do not require your comment." **Attribution:** Giglio, Louie.

CHAPTER 8: *"knowing, accepting, and being yourself—your best self— for God's glory." And* "thinking less of yourself than you ought to or thinking more of yourself than you ought to." **Attribution:** Shirer, P. (2005). He Speaks to Me. Nashville, Tennessee. Lifeway Press.

CHAPTER 10: Paraphrase: "He chose to walk in the direction of restoration and forgiveness towards the Father. That's when he had a life altering encounter with the one true God. You see, Jacob had his forefather's faith in the past, but was it his own faith? After Jacob wrestled with the Almighty, he was given the new name of Israel and was blessed." **Attribution:** Martin, Dena Johnson. (2014). How Wrestling with God will Change You Forever. Crosswalk.com

CHAPTER 10: "Sanctification is the act or process of acquiring sanctity, of being made or becoming holy. It is a gift given through the power of God to a person or thing which is then considered sacred or set apart." **Attribution:** Wikipedia

Made in the USA
Monee, IL
18 September 2020